Real Estate Brokerage: A Management Guide

Workbook

Ninth Edition

This publication is designed to provide accurate and authoritative information in regard to the subject matter covered. It is sold with the understanding that the publisher is not engaged in rendering legal, accounting, or other professional advice. If legal advice or other expert assistance is required, the services of a competent professional should be sought.

President: Dr. Andrew Temte
Executive Director, Real Estate Education: Melissa Kleeman-Moy
Development Editor: Rosita Hernandez

REAL ESTATE BROKERAGE: A MANAGEMENT GUIDE WORKBOOK
NINTH EDITION
©2017 Kaplan, Inc.
Published by DF Institute, Inc., d/b/a Dearborn Real Estate Education
332 Front St. S., Suite 501
La Crosse, WI 54601

Printed in the United States of America
First revision, July 2018
ISBN: 978-1-4754-5198-6

Contents

Introduction

This workbook has been designed to supplement *Real Estate Brokerage: A Management Guide*, Ninth Edition. That textbook is a manual to help you prepare for the tasks and responsibilities of running a brokerage business and supervising the people who work for the company.

In this workbook, we have prepared tools to assist you in successfully completing your course. Each chapter in the textbook has its counterpart here. In the workbook, each chapter includes the following:

- **Key terms**—important vocabulary identified from each chapter
- **Learning objectives**—several basic objectives you should be able to accomplish once you've mastered the material in each chapter
- **Chapter overview**—a synopsis of the general topics covered in the textbook
- **Quizzes**—20 multiple-choice questions that are designed to help you recall and review key points that were made in each chapter of the textbook

At the end of the workbook you'll find a complete answer key for the chapter quizzes. Each correct answer is followed by a page reference to the main textbook and a rationale, where the reasoning behind the answer is explained.

We hope that this workbook helps you enjoy your journey toward excellence in real estate brokerage leadership. Good luck!

CHAPTER

The Challenge
of Change

■ **KEY TERMS**

consumer-driven model   Internet Data Exchange   rightsizing
core services   (IDX)   supplier model
downsizing   multiple listing services
                                 (MLS)

■ **LEARNING OBJECTIVES**   *When you have completed this chapter, you will be able to*

■ **discuss** the effects of the economic environment on businesses and
consumers; and
■ **describe** the evolution of practices in the real estate business and **discuss**
trends that can alter business models for real estate companies, MLSs, and
professional organizations in the future.

CHAPTER OVERVIEW

History teaches powerful lessons about economic forces over which companies
have little control. Managers must look at the big picture of that economic environment and consider what were, what are, and what will be the events framed in
that picture to make wise decisions for their companies. Companies cannot continue to do the same things the same way and expect different results, especially
when the world around them is different.

The fundamental business of real estate has been to bring buyers and tenants
together with sellers and landlords to facilitate transactions. Brokers banded
together to form multiple listing services (MLSs) to facilitate the exchange of

property information. Consumers relied on brokers to guide transactions and provide information, especially about property listings.

Today information is power, the hot commodity in the marketplace served up by the internet. The internet also challenges the real estate industry's model that has controlled that information.

The marketplace is no longer geocentric, and the workforce and consumer populations are more culturally and generationally diverse. These factors challenge real estate companies to learn new ways to manage their workforces and serve consumers, and do so within increasing financial pressures and regulatory oversight that challenges traditional business models.

Consumers are also challenged by financial pressures. Job layoffs, damaged credit, and record amounts of student-loan debt have made the American dream of homeownership unattainable. For some consumers, the less permanent feature of renting is also more suitable for their lifestyles.

Considering all of these factors, companies must look at all the industry's traditional practices and make wise decisions about how to serve consumers in the future.

- What role will the real estate company play in the real estate transaction?
- What are the core services for a company?
- What role will multilists play?
- How will listing information be managed?
- What role will the industry's professional organizations play?
- What will the model be for a real estate company and its offices?
- Who will be the company's leaders?
- What will be the American dream of the future?

These are provocative questions but essential ones to consider for a company to make money, or even survive. The key to success is a willingness to look outside the real estate industry and learn how business organizations function in general.

CHAPTER 1 QUIZ

1. Which of the following is the MOST accurate description of today's house-seeking consumers?
   a. Little diversity
   b. More diversity
   c. Little interest in owning a home
   d. More men searching for a home

2. How did the subprime mortgage problem affect the U.S. economy?
   a. Housing prices decreased.
   b. Home equity increased.
   c. Stock market crash stimulated interest in real estate investment.
   d. It created jobs in the construction industry.

3. Real estate companies are different from other business enterprises because they
   a. make their own products.
   b. have no control over the products they sell.
   c. are less regulated by the government.
   d. have little contact with the average consumer.

4. What is the key factor that has driven real estate companies to ask, "What is our role?"
   a. Aging population
   b. More demands by Asians and Hispanics
   c. Evolving role of the internet
   d. Investigations by the Department of Justice

5. The internet has changed the real estate industry into
   a. a brick-and-mortar business.
   b. the realm of social services.
   c. construction venues.
   d. an information business.

6. What type of business model do consumers of today expect and demand?
   a. Supplier controls the selection of products and services offered
   b. A geocentric market with little or no input from a larger market
   c. Products and services tailored to consumer demand
   d. One-size-fits all service models

7. Some consumers are willing to purchase and pay only for services they want. As a result, real estate companies have
   a. adopted alternative pricing models.
   b. bundled their services into one package.
   c. increased transaction-based fees.
   d. restricted their core services.

8. What is the primary reason that real estate companies continue to support fixed real estate office locations?
   a. Consumers demand attractive office space.
   b. State regulations require fixed office locations.
   c. Real estate licensees expect to work in an attractive office.
   d. Companies can attract better quality listings and buyers.

9. What is the advantage of hiring sales agents as employees as opposed to hiring them as independent contractors?
   a. Employees cost less.
   b. The senior management team will have less supervisory responsibilities.
   c. Management has more control over sales activities.
   d. More people can be hired, thus increasing sales.

10. Companies, including real estate offices, often suffer from an "age divide," which refers to
    a. traditional 35-year "gold watch" retirements.
    b. the gap between the youthful senior management and older sales staff.
    c. the gap between the older entrenched senior management and lower-level younger people.
    d. the melting pot of cultures and generations.

11. What consumer goal that impacts the real estate industry has changed as a result of the Great Recession?
    a. Preference for homeownership
    b. Preference for rental housing
    c. Low expectation for property appreciation
    d. Expectation that their lives will be better than previous generation

12. With regard to changes in the marketplace, real estate regulators are typically
    a. reactive.
    b. proactive.
    c. unresponsive.
    d. heavy-handed.

13. Which of the following groups is MOST likely to be in real estate office upper management?
    a. Hispanics
    b. Asians
    c. Baby boomers
    d. Generation Y

14. What was the power of traditional multiple listing systems (MLSs)?
    a. Only members had access to the information.
    b. Sellers controlled who received information about their listings.
    c. Nonmembers had access but only upon specific request.
    d. Members agreed to limit cooperation fees.

15. What is a problem with Internet Data Exchanges (IDXs)?
    a. Allow consumers to view many listings
    b. Exclude nonmembers from accessing the listings
    c. Allow third-party internet companies to sell leads to companies' own listings
    d. No standardized format for updating listing information

16. Decisions about access to real estate listings are now made by
    a. real estate brokers.
    b. affiliate licensees who take the listing.
    c. local multiple listing services.
    d. owners whose properties are for sale.

17. Who determines what the consumer receives in a take-it-or-leave-it business model?
    a. The consumer
    b. The supplier
    c. The regulator
    d. General business practices

18. What group is quickly becoming the largest minority?
    a. Asians
    b. African Americans
    c. Hispanics
    d. Native Americans

19. Real estate companies that have expanded the meaning of *core services* may now assist consumers in all of the following EXCEPT
    a. job placement for a spouse.
    b. day care for a child or elderly parent.
    c. handyman services.
    d. verifying the accuracy of seller property disclosures.

20. What was the original primary reason for choosing a location for a real estate office?
    a. Draw for foot traffic
    b. Easy to erect large signage
    c. Denote market share
    d. Vanity of broker/owner

CHAPTER 2

Leadership

accountability	ego	leadership
decisiveness	empathy	management
delegation	integrity	team building

■ **LEARNING OBJECTIVES** *When you have completed this chapter, you will be able to*

- **identify** essential character traits of a leader;
- **analyze** leadership qualities that affect people's perceptions of a leader; and
- **discuss** how leaders use their positions to command a following, **distinguish** the ways in which managers and leaders view their roles in an organization, and **discuss** what steps a person can take to develop as a leader.

CHAPTER OVERVIEW

The essence of leadership is the ability to influence other people and persuade them to follow. Leaders are able to command a following because they have certain character traits—integrity, honesty, trustworthiness, loyalty, and respect—that demonstrate they are worthy of allegiance and will use the power of the position responsibly.

Leaders also possess certain qualities that demonstrate they can do an admirable job of guiding us. Qualities that are generally attributed to leaders include the following:

- **Vision**—the long-range, independent thinking that looks for new or more inspired ways to do things; the quality that blazes trails, takes risks, and inspires others with passion and enthusiasm
- **Ego and empathy**—the self-confident presence and self-respect (ego) that respects the thoughts, feelings, and abilities of others and acknowledges their worth (empathy)
- **Team building**—the quality that draws people together and builds coalitions to stimulate creative thinking and problem solving, build consensus, resolve or manage conflict, and achieve support for what the leader wants to do
- **Decisiveness**—the ability to take charge and provide direction to frame definitive courses of action
- **Accountability**—the quality that takes responsibility for the consequences of that person's actions and decisions and those of the people the person supervises
- **Delegation**—the transfer of authority to another person to do a job and trust someone else to do a job for which the delegator is ultimately responsible, which also means giving up control and conferring the right to make commitments and use resources

Managers are work focused, while leaders are people focused. Many people have inherent qualities that can make them effective leaders. But leadership qualities can also be developed.

- How do leaders and managers approach their jobs in an organization differently?
- What are the benefits of leadership versus management in an organization?
- How do managers become leaders?

CHAPTER 2 QUIZ

1. A person is accepted in a leadership position when the followers
   a. trust that the person will use power and influence responsibly.
   b. expect that the person will answer to certain parties.
   c. anticipate that the person will act according to specific demands.
   d. assume that the person will change positions when expedient.

2. All of the following are revered character traits in a leader *EXCEPT*
   a. integrity.
   b. honesty.
   c. duplicity.
   d. trustworthiness.

3. What causes people to stop being loyal to their leader?
   a. The leader uses knowledge for truthful and honorable purposes.
   b. People's personal needs are no longer being met.
   c. The leader is disliked but accomplishes required goals.
   d. People agree with leader's changed objectives.

4. How are codes for ethical and moral behavior developed?
   a. Determined by state and federal law
   b. Developed by hit or miss decisions
   c. Established by company policies and procedures
   d. Influenced by family, culture, religion, and society

5. Regarding the character of a leader, generally, people
   a. will follow an unethical person as long as they can make money.
   b. must have faith that their leader's decisions are always right.
   c. need to find a correlation between their own belief system and that of their leader.
   d. must love their leaders.

6. What is a leader's ultimate abuse of power?
   a. Use of coercion to gain compliance
   b. Treats individuals fairly and with dignity
   c. Unwillingness to compromise for personal gain
   d. Willingness to stand by necessary, but difficult decisions

7. What action is *MOST* likely from a self-assured leader?
   a. Do what needs to be done to reach the leader's goals
   b. Acknowledge the self-worth of followers
   c. Sacrifice the interests of the followers to make the leader look good
   d. Demand sacrifices from those who are supporters of the leader

8. All of the following characteristics are valuable for a leader *EXCEPT*
   a. being willing to take care of others.
   b. being compassionate.
   c. being open-minded.
   d. resolutely sticking to any decision already made.

9. Leaders should have a healthy sense of ego because they must be able to
   a. be egomaniacs.
   b. use their egos to build themselves up in the eyes of others.
   c. use their weaknesses to build themselves up in the eyes of others.
   d. use their confidence and self-respect for the benefit of others.

10. How do MOST people respond to the character of a leader?
    a. Will follow an unethical person as long as the leader can make money
    b. Must have faith that their leader's decisions are always right
    c. Need to find a correlation between their own belief systems and that of their leader
    d. Must find something to love about their leader

11. What is the benefit, if any, for the leader to encourage team building?
    a. Very little, as it distracts from working to pursue individual needs
    b. Very beneficial when it stimulates ideas and an appreciation for the rewards that are possible in collective efforts
    c. No benefit if working with real estate agents who are generally independent contractors
    d. Some benefit when people are drawn into activities on behalf of the organization, the goals of the leader, or both

12. What value, if any, is there for a leader being decisive?
    a. Little value because it is not a characteristic that is admired in a leader
    b. Some value because it means being able to make snap decisions on the fly
    c. Great value when the leader is willing to make decisions and accept the risk involved
    d. Required value because the leader must interject a decision into every situation that arises

13. Leaders can handle responsibility and accountability by
    a. readily acknowledging their errors in judgment.
    b. delegating the responsibility for their mistakes to others.
    c. sitting back rather than admitting their responsibility.
    d. fearing a loss of respect if they acknowledge their errors in judgment.

14. An affiliated licensee in a brokerage of 60 affiliated licensees is charged with a violation of the state's real estate license law. Who is MOST responsible for the actions of the affiliated licensee?
    a. The team leader
    b. The broker of the large office
    c. The client who hired the brokerage
    d. The unlicensed partners of the broker

15. What is MOST important when a leader delegates authority to another?
    a. Retain enough control to ensure a favorable outcome
    b. Take credit for favorable outcomes, but not for unfavorable ones
    c. Confer complete authority, that is, the right to direct the job that needs to be done
    d. Describe in detail how each delegated task should be performed

16. When the leader makes a decision to delegate the completion of a task to another, the leader
    a. may assign tasks to unskilled people to see if they can rise to the challenge.
    b. should only include those of his own group without regard for the welfare of others.
    c. should take credit for the accomplishments of the task.
    d. must identify the right person for the specific work.

17. What are the characteristics of an effective leader?
    a. Encourage others to grow and develop to their highest potential
    b. Refuse to share credit with other people for accomplishments of the organization
    c. Be consumed with her position of authority
    d. Be reactive with an eye on short-term objectives

18. One difference between a manager and a leader is that a leader
    a. proactively designs systems with an eye on long-term success.
    b. works well within well-defined systems.
    c. works as a caretaker of traditional formulas to keep the organization on track.
    d. avoids any deviations from established agreed-upon formulas.

19. Which of the following is a characteristic of an effective manager?
    a. People focused
    b. Do things to keep business on course
    c. Develop the talents of others
    d. Design systems and processes to support the people

20. What is a key factor in leadership development?
    a. Must be born with leadership qualities
    b. Assume authority when named as the leader
    c. Learn leadership through observation and introspection
    d. Avoid distraction through involvement with the wider community

CHAPTER 3

Management Skills

LEARNING OBJECTIVES

When you have completed this chapter, you will be able to

- **identify** management styles and how managers use their authority in each style;
- **discuss** the skills managers need to motivate people and manage human behavior in the workplace and how the manager's behavior affects the dynamics of a diverse workplace; and
- **develop** a plan for a successful transition into a managerial position.

CHAPTER OVERVIEW

A manager's job is to get things done through other people. Managers do this by being effective leaders and developing the skills needed to guide human behavior in the workplace.

Management styles—dictatorial, autocratic, participatory, and laissez-faire—are essentially the ways managers provide direction and use authority, depending on how managers view their roles and what they think about workers. Philosophies have changed over time, with the participatory style being the one that most closely resembles the leadership expected of today's managers.

Managers have many duties but they all relate to one thing—motivating people. This is the aspect of management that requires certain skills to manage human behavior—observation, communication, interpersonal skills, team building, decision making, negotiation and conflict resolution, and time management. Managers need these skills to guide a workforce with diverse skills, attitudes, and viewpoints while also dealing with the personal demands of the job.

The common strategy in the business world of promoting the best technicians into managerial roles is also prevalent in the real estate industry—good salespeople are often elevated to management positions. But people are often promoted out of the jobs they do best and then wither in administrative jobs. The job and the person have to be a good fit.

- Is a promotion a good thing for you?
- Are you suited for the job?
- How do you make the transition?

Being a sales manager after being a salesperson creates a unique set of challenges—learning to supervise others who do what the manager once did. In some companies, the job may require the person to both manage and sell—two roles that add to the challenges of being a manager.

CHAPTER 3 QUIZ

1. A property manager of a large firm requires detailed reports for every rental transaction and does not allow any variation. No one dares to question the broker's authority. What is the management style of this broker?
   a. Autocratic style
   b. Dictatorial style
   c. Laissez-faire style
   d. Participative style

2. The style of management in which the manager makes all decisions, shows concern for people, and enables them to feel secure is
   a. the autocratic style.
   b. the dictatorial style.
   c. the laissez-faire style.
   d. the participative style.

3. The style of management that promotes initiative and recognizes the value of the company's human resources is
   a. the autocratic style.
   b. the dictatorial style.
   c. the laissez-faire style.
   d. the participative style.

4. The style of management that is characterized by the manager's nonintervention and hands-off approach is
   a. the autocratic style.
   b. the dictatorial style.
   c. the laissez-faire style.
   d. the participative style.

5. To modify behavior, the manager should first identify the unacceptable behavior and then
   a. clearly describe the preferred behavior.
   b. issue an order that will correct the worker's behavior.
   c. correct each and every error as it is made.
   d. discuss the worker's incompetency.

6. An effective manager can encourage the right behavior by
   a. helping the offender memorize approved responses.
   b. developing an action plan.
   c. asking detailed questions.
   d. consulting a group of experts.

7. When evaluating people's behavior, it's important for the manager to
   a. ignore desirable behavior because people are doing what they're supposed to.
   b. praise the behavior that is desirable or acceptable.
   c. criticize the person who has stepped out of line.
   d. yell at a person so it's clear the manager is displeased about something that was done.

8. What do young adults in today's workforce expect?
   a. Quick feedback and identifiable displays of appreciation
   b. Little or no feedback until a project is completed
   c. Complete autonomy with little signs of appreciation
   d. Quiet and unassuming leaders

9. To effect lasting, positive behavioral changes, the manager should
   a. identify a person's annoying habits.
   b. clearly describe why the behavior is unacceptable.
   c. explain exactly what the offender should do differently.
   d. engage in follow up to hold the offender accountable for implementing the action plan.

10. It is very natural for a manager to label a person because of a particular trait or skill. When a manager has a preconceived notion about someone,
    a. this helps manage the person.
    b. this helps treat the person fairly.
    c. it's difficult to see the person as an individual.
    d. it takes less time for the manager to evaluate what the person does.

11. In today's real estate offices, managers are very likely supervising individuals
    a. with backgrounds very similar to that of the manager.
    b. with very homogenous backgrounds.
    c. whose profiles are significantly different from the managers'.
    d. who are very similar to the owner of the company.

12. What is the role of a leader who is managing discussions in an office of diverse individuals?
    a. Facilitator
    b. Director of opinion
    c. Mediator
    d. Constructive devil's advocate

13. How can a company properly acknowledge the diversity in the workforce?
    a. More tolerance for those who are similar to the manager's heritage
    b. Zero tolerance for sexual harassment
    c. Expect that everyone will be friends even outside the office
    d. Evaluations based on lifestyle and dress

14. To juggle work life with personal life, the manager must be able to
    a. expect subordinates to stay out of the way when stress levels are high.
    b. tell everyone when he is having a bad day personally.
    c. hide any personal issues and not allow them to interfere with office relationships.
    d. perform multiple duties and responsibilities with calm good humor.

15. How should a manager deal with stress?
    a. Work longer hours to get everything done
    b. Change attitudes or the situations that cause stress
    c. Take more courses to enhance professional competency
    d. Ignore personal stress and concentrate on the behavior of others

16. The real estate salesperson who has been promoted to management MOST likely needs additional training in
    a. state rules and regulations.
    b. advanced courses in listing and selling skills.
    c. using the internet to market properties more effectively.
    d. business and human resource management.

17. While predicting entrepreneurial skills is difficult, what is the one specific trait that does seem to stand out in predicting entrepreneurial success?
    a. Accountability
    b. Decisive decision-making skills
    c. Ability to delegate tasks
    d. Confidence and ability to build a successful business

18. What should a newly appointed manager do to gain cooperation from those who are supervised?
    a. Make decisions that are popular with everyone
    b. Remind subordinates that he was once one of them and understands what they are going through
    c. Just take over and do things that the manager knows she can do better
    d. Demonstrate genuine respect for the position and the people being supervised

19. Combining real estate activities and management requires that the new manager
    a. prioritize responsibilities.
    b. determine the number of hours that the manager will be paid.
    c. give up selling activities.
    d. work the best leads to have enough time to manage the other salespeople.

20. All of the following are reasons for being a full-time sales manager EXCEPT
    a. not competing with salespeople for business.
    b. not distracted by sales activities.
    c. more time for personal business.
    d. protects harmony in the office.

CHAPTER 4

Communications and Decision Making

■ **LEARNING OBJECTIVES**   *When you have completed this chapter, you will be able to*

- **identify** the essential components of good oral and written communications;
- **explain** how to make business writing effective;
- **compare** the advantages and disadvantages of various forms of electronic communication and **identify** the factors that lead to successful meetings and public speaking; and
- **discuss** the general types of decisions leaders make, the steps involved in making decisions, and the variables that affect the quality of decisions and their implementation.

CHAPTER OVERVIEW

Managers are vital information links with superiors, subordinates, and the external community. But they can be effective in that role only if they are effective communicators. Oral communication has numerous benefits—tone of voice, facial expressions, and body language—that add to the power of words people exchange. Because personal contact is diminishing in today's business world, managers have to communicate as effectively in writing as they do in person.

- How do you make your message reach your intended audience?
- How do you make sure the message you intend is the one people receive?

- What do you say about yourself in the way your message is written?
- How do you write for various media?

Effective communication also means picking the right forum for the purpose. Face-to-face or one-on-one exchanges are the most interactive forums and are clearly the most suitable for personal and personnel matters.

Technology offers numerous written venues—emails, blogs, texts, tweets, Microsoft Word documents, Adobe PDFs, and Microsoft PowerPoint presentations—each of which has certain advantages and disadvantages, which can create different confidentiality and legal issues. Managers must learn to pick the medium that suits the goal, the audience, and the nature of the message or writing that is being disseminated. The visual aspects of writing are as important as the words themselves, which means managers must learn to capture an audience's attention and persuade people to act and interact.

Business meetings still have their place, especially for sharing information with a number of people at the same time and engaging in controlled group discussions. But meetings are only worthwhile when they have a clearly defined purpose, give people a reason to attend, and are well planned and conducted properly. Learning to be a good public speaker also gives the manager the tools to conduct good meetings.

Good communications leads to good information gathering, which is essential for good decision making. Those decisions typically fall into one of four categories—entrepreneurial or institutional, corrective, resource, and mediation—each of which serves a different purpose. The classic model of decision making, involving a series of seven steps, is a very deliberate approach that intends to result in the most informed decision.

The quality of any decision, including one made on the spur of the moment, is directly related to the information, expertise, and personalities of the people making the decision. Many variables are involved. Once made, a decision must be implemented, which means communicating the decision and mobilizing the resources, processes, and procedures to support the decision.

CHAPTER 4 QUIZ

1. What is the primary disadvantage of email?
   a. Fewer opportunities to gather information
   b. Provides way to inexpensively and widely disseminate information
   c. Important information can get lost in the shuffle
   d. Shorter time to process the information

2. When should a manager schedule a private meeting?
   a. Information that affects everyone in the company
   b. Individual performance reviews
   c. A new ad campaign
   d. New trends in the industry

3. In which situation should the manager schedule a large meeting for everyone to attend?
   a. Individual performance reviews
   b. When imparting decisions that affect the entire company
   c. When the information affects only a couple of people
   d. Personal problems or disciplinary action affecting certain individuals

4. What is the BEST format to compile lasting information that can be edited and revised?
   a. Blogs
   b. Wikis
   c. Really Simple Syndication
   d. Loose-leaf notebooks

5. Which of the following catalogs content and becomes an instant messenger that alerts users to new information?
   a. Blogs
   b. Wikis
   c. Email
   d. Really Simple Syndication

6. One way to encourage attendance at an office meeting is to
   a. regularly and consistently schedule meetings.
   b. schedule the times randomly to keep everyone on their toes.
   c. publicize the agenda.
   d. regularly run overtime since there are so many topics to discuss.

7. What format should the manager use when he needs to control the delivery of important information as well as to identify how the information is received?
   a. Email the information
   b. Circulate a memo that must be signed by each person
   c. Hold a face-to-face meeting
   d. Send out text messages

8. Which action is LEAST likely to deliver an effective message at a business meeting?
   a. Speaking off the cuff
   b. Picking the right topic
   c. Practicing in advance
   d. Choosing humor wisely

9. When using electronic communication, which of the following is the number one rule?
   a. Respond quickly
   b. Read before hitting send
   c. Think about legal liability
   d. Avoid any information that might be considered controversial

10. What is a distinctive quality of classic decision making?
    a. Putting out fires
    b. "Shooting from the hip"
    c. Waiting until all the facts are known
    d. Following a set of rational and logical steps

11. Why do people generally dislike attending business meetings?
    a. They dislike the other participants.
    b. People are afraid that they will be subject to a performance review.
    c. The information should have been delivered by a memo or report.
    d. People hate surprises.

12. A manager must deliver the news that the company is going to close an office, relocate several staff, and let others go. What is the BEST way for the manager to deliver this news to all 125 affiliate licensees?
    a. Send an email to everyone so that they get the information at the same time
    b. Schedule face-to-face meetings with those who will be most affected by the move
    c. Tell a few people and ask them to pass on the information
    d. Pass the responsibility to your secretary

13. Written communications are preferable to oral ones when the manager
    a. has a lot of detailed information to impart.
    b. does not want to confront a person face-to-face.
    c. needs feedback.
    d. does not have time to talk to a person about an important issue.

14. What is one negative part of publishing a meeting agenda ahead of the actual meeting?
    a. It forces the presenter to plan remarks ahead of time.
    b. It makes more efficient use of the actual meeting time.
    c. People can form opinions before hearing all the information and come prepared with their remarks.
    d. People can decide to avoid the meeting if they don't like the topic.

15. What is the key to effective public speaking?
    a. Telling people what the manager thinks they want to hear
    b. Preparing the presentation the hour before
    c. Winging it
    d. Good writing, rewritten, and rehearsed

16. All of the following should be included in a presentation EXCEPT
    a. explain the general outline of the talk.
    b. apologize for not being a more forceful public speaker.
    c. present the material in a precise manner.
    d. review the topics that you just covered.

17. Decisions that resolve problems, crises, or dilemmas are referred to as
    a. entrepreneurial decisions.
    b. corrective decisions.
    c. resource decisions.
    d. mediation decisions.

18. What is solved by an entrepreneurial decision?
    a. Significant strategic directions, policies, or fundamental systems
    b. Problems, dilemmas, or crises
    c. Allocation of personnel or money
    d. Negotiated solutions

19. What is the very first step when faced with a decision-making dilemma?
    a. Develop alternatives
    b. Evaluate the outcome
    c. Select an appropriate alternative
    d. Define the situation

20. An announcement should not only communicate a decision but also
    a. encourage everyone to second-guess the decision.
    b. enhance the likelihood that it will be implemented.
    c. focus attention on the format of the delivery.
    d. justify and defend the decision.

CHAPTER

5

Analyzing the Business Environment

consumer confidence   gross domestic product   inflationary cycles

demographics   housing market

■ **LEARNING OBJECTIVES**   *When you have completed this chapter, you will be able to*

■ **discuss** the importance of analyzing the business climate in the local area and **identify** economic factors that affect the real estate business in the local area;

■ **discuss** the effect of public policies on the local business environment; and

■ **identify** sociological factors and demographics that affect the business of real estate in the local area.

CHAPTER OVERVIEW

A business plan is only as good as the analysis of the business environment and the assumptions made about the future. That analysis must include quantifiable evidence or the cold, hard facts that establish credibility for the plan. Economists and business analysts follow a number of key economic indicators: gross domestic product, inflationary cycles, consumer confidence, and the housing market. An analysis of each of these reveals various aspects of the economy that indicate strength, weakness, and trends that can have future impacts.

Public policy makers make decisions that ultimately affect the business community and real estate in particular. An analysis of the business environment answers several questions.

- What is the climate for stimulating business and job growth?
- What tax policies and government regulations affect corporate development?
- What is the climate for economic growth and development in the area?
- What environmental issues affect real estate in the area?
- What government regulations affect real estate practices in particular?

The social or demographic environment is the people factor that affects virtually every aspect of a company's business, from its workforce to its clientele. Demographic profiles are particularly helpful for tailoring products and services, delivery systems, and advertising programs that suit the available pool of potential consumers and affect the demand for housing. A number of resources provide the data to analyze the effect of

- age and generational demographics,
- household composition,
- population shifts, and
- ethnic and cultural demographics.

The U.S. Census Bureau also projects trends that are especially useful for deciding what the company needs to be doing in the future to suit the demographics.

CHAPTER 5 QUIZ

1. What is the broadest indicator(s) of the strength of the economy?
    a. Local employment statistics
    b. Gross domestic product
    c. Long-term interest rates
    d. Broker's profits for the most recent year

2. A healthy economy should generate
    a. a low, stable inflation rate.
    b. a low, overheated inflation rate.
    c. a high, stable inflation rate.
    d. a high, overheated inflation rate.

3. What can the Federal Reserve do to curb inflation?
    a. Lower interest rates
    b. Increase the money supply
    c. Require larger down payments for loans
    d. Increase interest rates

4. A large spread between short-term interest rates and long-term bond rates indicates that the Federal Reserve is
    a. attempting to fuel the economy.
    b. attempting to cool the economy.
    c. discouraging people from spending.
    d. encouraging an inflationary spiral.

5. What was the effect during the Great Recession of the lowest interest rates in decades and the credit boom that occurred in the previous few years?
    a. Slowed down the housing market
    b. Fostered subprime mortgage loans that are now in default
    c. Increased number of corporate takeover plans
    d. Increased credit availability

6. What is one of the problems of business planning during periods of stable inflation?
    a. Easy to be lulled into a false sense of security
    b. Hard to be optimistic
    c. Easy to read economic indicators
    d. Difficult to make timely adjustments

7. What influences consumer confidence?
    a. Employment stability
    b. Convincing real estate advertising
    c. Rising interest rates
    d. Additional environmental regulations

8. The essential challenge in economic growth and development is
    a. stressing existing infrastructures.
    b. increasing the number of entitlement programs.
    c. balancing benefits with costs.
    d. eliminating declining neighborhoods.

9. The measures of consumer pricing index include the prices of
    a. food.
    b. fuel.
    c. housing.
    d. energy.

10. When gauging consumer confidence, on what factors are dealers in less-frequently purchased items (such as vehicles, home appliances, and houses) MOST dependent?
    a. Long-term sales trends
    b. Short-term sales trends
    c. Trends in monthly sales
    d. Job growth predictions

11. Consumer confidence is NOT ALWAYS affected by
    a. job security.
    b. sufficient wages to support cost of living.
    c. minimal debt.
    d. low interest rates.

12. What is one of the indicators of the strength of the economy?
    a. Housing market
    b. Availability and cost of appliances
    c. Number of alternative mortgage loans
    d. Number of people over the age of 65

13. What is the effect of environmental issues on the real estate community?
    a. Little effect in most parts of the country
    b. Major effect on most business planners
    c. Rarely intersect with private development
    d. Minimal legal liability on real estate practitioners

14. The real estate community has *ALWAYS* supported
    a. development with additional environmental restrictions.
    b. increased regulatory intervention to stimulate development.
    c. using land development to eliminate social problems.
    d. private property rights.

15. How do the interests of the public and the rights of private property owners affect each other?
    a. Restrictions that protect the public also enhance the private owner's enjoyment of the real estate.
    b. Restrictions that protect the public also usually result in lower costs when the private owner wants to develop his real estate.
    c. Environmental issues that protect the public usually do not have an adverse financial impact on the private owner.
    d. Regulations that service the public interest can erode the rights of the private owner.

16. All of the following disclosures are generally required in residential real estate transactions *EXCEPT*
    a. disclosures of agency.
    b. disclosures of property conditions.
    c. disclosures of environmental substances.
    d. disclosures of racial diversity of the neighborhood.

17. Which group has reached its maximum earning potential and remains a driving force in the real estate market?
    a. Generation X
    b. Generation Y
    c. Baby boomers
    d. Immigrants

18. To meet the needs of foreign-born buyers, real estate companies should invest in
    a. teaching English as a foreign language.
    b. financial planning.
    c. cultural diversity training.
    d. anti-discrimination instruction.

19. How well a real estate company performs is a function of how well management
    a. tolerates diversity.
    b. analyzes factors in the local environment that have a bearing on its operations.
    c. can respond to lower prices charged by the competition.
    d. correctly predicts the next wave of job layoffs or job creation.

20. What are the primary reasons for population shifts from one part of the country to another?
    a. Employment opportunities
    b. Desire for cultural diversity
    c. Lower home prices
    d. Area's tolerance for diversity

CHAPTER

6

Analyzing the Market

■ **KEY TERMS**

agency disclosure	dual agency	nonagency
buyer representation	market share	seller representation
designated agency	niche markets	single agency

■ **LEARNING OBJECTIVES**   *When you have completed this chapter, you will be able to*

- **identify** key aspects of the marketplace that affect a real estate company's business and **discuss** the effect of the law of agency on the consumer and a company's practices;
- **explain** what a market analysis reveals about the company's target markets and the company's competition; and
- **explain** how a market analysis is used to tailor what a company does.

CHAPTER OVERVIEW

A market analysis converts what we *believe* about the business of real estate into hard data about who the consumers are, where they are located, what services they need, and where they go to get those services. This analysis is essential for assessing opportunities in the marketplace and determining what a company needs to be doing (and cease doing) to be a viable enterprise in the future.

There are a variety of ways to look at the marketplace—including geographic markets and service markets—to gather information about consumers and the company's competitors. This analysis helps makes the cost-versus-benefits decisions about MLSs, referrals, and relocation networks and the types of property or scope of services the company should pursue.

Another way to look at the marketplace is through the prism of the law of agency.

■ Who does the company represent?
■ What company procedures are needed to support that decision?
■ What services do sellers and buyers want from the broker?

Each state has specific requirements for serving clients and customers and the contracts or documents that brokerage companies use. But all states require some form of agency disclosure.

The final piece of a market analysis is an analysis of the company and how it fits into the marketplace. This answers several basic questions.

■ How well do the company's services suit what the consumer wants?
■ What is the company's market share?
■ What is the business potential in the company's target markets?
■ How does the company stack up against the competition?

The answers lead to decisions about what the company needs to be doing or cease doing so that it can direct resources to more productive efforts. This also requires a critical look at the internal operations—the structure, systems, and processes—and how those contribute to the efficiency and effectiveness of the enterprise.

CHAPTER 6 QUIZ

1. Using a market-driven approach for a company's operations
   a. helps ensure that services the consumers want are being provided.
   b. is an outdated business philosophy.
   c. is costly in relation to the benefits the company derives.
   d. ignores the needs of the customers.

2. One of the primary advantages to consumers who use the internet for real estate information is that they
   a. can be more participatory in the pursuit and evaluation of information.
   b. do not have to work with any particular agent.
   c. have a better reason to upgrade their computer systems.
   d. can work with more than one agent at a time.

3. Multiple listing services (MLSs) are becoming
   a. obsolete in today's practice.
   b. more useful to buyers than sellers.
   c. broader information systems.
   d. more regulated by the state's licensing authority.

4. Which of the following is a way that a brokerage firm can expand the geographic scope of its services?
   a. Niche marketing
   b. Buyer brokerage
   c. An affiliation with referral networks
   d. Cost-of-living comparisons

5. Before making a decision to enter into an intercity referral network, the broker should determine
   a. a cost-versus-benefits equation.
   b. how effective the referral program will be to develop new business from immigrants.
   c. whether or not the referral program will work with minorities.
   d. if it is necessary to use a third-party equity contractor.

6. A disadvantage of joining an intercity referral network could be
   a. the potential for increased clientele.
   b. the benefit of name recognition.
   c. the competitive advantage in the local market.
   d. the expectation of providing a myriad of nontraditional services for a corporation and its transferees.

7. A broker does business in a town with a population of 5,000. The broker lists and sells residential listings, leases apartments in multifamily buildings, and occasionally lists commercial real estate as well. This broker is
   a. a generalist.
   b. a specialist.
   c. a niche marketer.
   d. a high-quality individual.

8. One of the drawbacks to concentrating on a specialized market niche is
   a. the potential volume of business that is possible.
   b. the specialized skill needed to serve the market.
   c. the markets the competition serves.
   d. putting all of your eggs in one basket.

9. Serving real estate investors requires a broad base knowledge of
   a. fair housing laws.
   b. tax laws and those governing exchanges.
   c. cultural diversity.
   d. current housing trends.

10. What describes real estate counseling?
    a. Niche market that requires a sophisticated analysis of an investor's circumstances
    b. Service provided to first-time buyers to assist them in making an informed house-buying decision
    c. Generalist approach to helping sellers be less involved emotionally in the sale of their homes
    d. Specialized market that focuses on successful 1031 exchanges

11. When an affiliate licensee takes a listing, the broker appoints that licensee to represent the seller. The broker appoints another licensee in the same company to represent the buyer. This is an example of
    a. single agency.
    b. designated agency.
    c. informed clients who agree to dual representation.
    d. nonagency.

12. A broker who does NOT represent either party in the same transaction is practicing
    a. single agency.
    b. dual agency.
    c. designated agency.
    d. nonagency.

13. Who is ultimately responsible for deciding the agency services a brokerage firm is going to provide and who will receive client-level and customer-level services?
    a. Principal broker
    b. Sales managers
    c. Individual sales agents
    d. Consumers

14. Although each type of listing agreement has advantages and disadvantages, an exclusive-right-to-sell listing is generally viewed to be preferable because
    a. the seller can sell the property without being obligated to pay a commission.
    b. only the broker who sells the property earns a commission.
    c. it eliminates controversy about whether the listing broker is entitled to commission.
    d. the seller does not have to pay a commission if a buyer's representative sells the property.

15. The state requires that the listing licensee explain representation options to the seller. This discussion is known as
    a. discovery process.
    b. due diligence.
    c. persistence to detail.
    d. agency disclosure.

16. One of the major reasons for studying the demographics of the population and the number of various types of properties in the area is to
    a. identify the potential for business for a company and its services.
    b. criticize the competition.
    c. qualify for affiliation with a relocation company.
    d. guarantee business when recruiting salespeople.

17. One indication of a company's success in challenging the competition is an ongoing analysis of its
    a. location.
    b. market share.
    c. affiliations.
    d. number of customer services offered.

18. A broker wants to expand operations by affiliating with a national franchise company. Which of the following will provide information that may help make a final decision?
    a. Take a poll of the broker's affiliate licensees
    b. Talk with an attorney who specializes in franchising
    c. Visit with brokers who were formerly part of that particular franchise
    d. Ask the broker's accountant to scrutinize the franchise offering

19. Before making an expansion decision, a broker should consider all of the following EXCEPT
    a. possible affiliations.
    b. marketing strategies.
    c. ability to attract and retain salespeople.
    d. offering free home warranties.

20. Scrutinizing the current status of your company is MOST useful when planning its future because
    a. the competition knows more about the company than you do.
    b. it's difficult to develop realistic plans without knowing about the company's operations.
    c. it will probably be necessary to restructure the organization.
    d. this minimizes resentment by the salespeople.

CHAPTER

Developing a Plan

3-5yr. Blueprint On

■ **KEY TERMS**

done last but on 1st page

business plan
contingency plan
executive summary ←
general objectives

goals
long-range plan
mission statement

situational analysis
strategies
tactics

■ **LEARNING OBJECTIVES**   *When you have completed this chapter, you will be able to*

■ **describe** the purpose of a strategic plan;
■ **discuss** the components of a strategic plan, **define** the mission of an organization and the purpose of a mission statement, and **explain** the characteristics of properly written goals and strategies; and
■ **describe** the planning process for implementing a business plan.

CHAPTER OVERVIEW

The purpose of a long-range plan is to enable an organization to be a meaningful specific instead of a wandering generality. A plan allows a company to direct its human and financial resources to selected activities that will yield the greatest return on investment. But the plan has to provide specific directions—general objectives, goals, strategies, and tactics—that support the mission of the organization. Planning answers:

■ What does the company need to do?
■ How does the company intend to accomplish that?
■ How does the company know whether it's doing what it set out to do?

Planning is the fundamental activity from which virtually every business decision flows. But a strategic plan is only as good as the situational analysis that supports assumptions about the future, the achievability of the goals and strategies, and the level of commitment to implementing the plan. In addition to long-range planning, companies engage in a variety of other planning activities: yearly business plans, tactical plans, and contingency plans.

A major benefit of planning is the process itself or the discussions that ensue as various viewpoints, creative ideas, and possible solutions are shared. This is a participatory exercise that fosters teamwork and engages people who have a stake in the outcomes in ways that enhance implementation. Once developed, a plan is committed to writing and assembled into a usable document. That generally includes an executive summary (the condensed version of the plan) and a summary of the situation analysis, which provides the rationale for the plan.

CHAPTER 7 QUIZ

1. The purpose of business planning is to
   a. satisfy the state's licensing authority.
   b. do what management books tell you to do.
   c. protect traditional activities of the organization.
   d. direct the company's human and financial resources properly.

2. What is the value of a good business plan?
   a. Provides specific guidance about what to do and how to do it
   b. Is a road map from which it cannot deviate
   c. Models its operations to be the same as the competition
   d. Operates the same as it did in the past

3. The MOST likely key factor for the success of a business plan will be
   a. the professional planners hired by the broker to write the plan.
   b. the accountant who worked up the financials for the business plan.
   c. the manager who proposed the plan to the broker.
   d. the input from people at various levels in the organization.

4. Once the business plan is developed, the plan
   a. can be completely ignored.
   b. can be ignored when circumstances change that make it unworkable.
   c. should be implemented throughout the organization.
   d. should be implemented from the top down.

5. The broker wrote a business plan, but six months later, a hurricane destroyed much of the housing and the economy dramatically changed. In this situation, the broker
   a. should ignore the original business plan and write a new one.
   b. should make adjustments and set more achievable goals.
   c. can forget about planning because the economy is too unpredictable.
   d. should wing it until the housing market stabilizes.

6. A long-range, general, or strategic plan typically spans
   a. one year.
   b. two years.
   c. three to five years.
   d. five or more years.

7. What is the brief statement that outlines the organization's fundamental purpose for existing?
   a. General objectives
   b. Overall goals
   c. Strategies
   d. Mission statement

8. In a business plan, the general objectives become the organization's
   a. priorities during the timeframe of the plan.
   b. plans for what to do if the economy changes.
   c. outline for how to achieve profitability.
   d. foundation on which the business enterprise is built.

9. Knowing profitability allows an organization to
   a. recognize if the organization must borrow money to continue operations.
   b. validate the way that the organization is operating in pursuit of its goals.
   c. borrow more capital for expansion.
   d. illustrate that real estate licensees should join the firm.

10. An organization's mission statement is, "The company is in business to be successful." This mission statement
    a. says exactly what the business expects to do.
    b. states where the business expects to be in the future.
    c. states the purpose for the business to exist.
    d. says that business hopes to survive, but says little more.

11. Which of the following is a characteristic of a successful goal?
    a. Vague
    b. Measurable
    c. Indeterminate
    d. Indefinite

12. What process lays out a methodology for accomplishing goals?
    a. Contingency planning
    b. Strategic planning
    c. Alternative forecasting
    d. Production accomplishment

13. The broker has decided that the commercial division of her company is not profitable because other larger, more funded companies are doing the commercial transactions. In what section of the business plan, if any, should this phase-out be addressed?
    a. Strategy part of the plan
    b. The mission statement
    c. Individual goals
    d. Nowhere, because it is not necessary to plan for discontinuing a market or service

14. In which order should the components of a plan be written?
    a. Goal, strategy, general objective
    b. Mission statement, general objective, contingencies
    c. General objective, goal, strategy
    d. Mission statement, contingencies, goals

15. The broker wants to establish a relocation department. Which of the following is a strategy to accomplish this?
    a. Make the necessary preparations and plan allocation of resources to that end
    b. Increase the number of referrals from corporate clients
    c. Establish alternatives in case the new enterprise does not make money
    d. Create the best referral network in the geographical area

16. What kind of planning provides alternatives for the organization in the case of certain events?
    a. Short-range planning
    b. Contingency planning
    c. Activity planning
    d. Tactical planning

17. What is usually written last but included first in the formal planning document?
    a. Mission statement
    b. Executive summary
    c. General strategies
    d. Long-term goals

18. What is necessary if the business plan is to be successfully implemented?
    a. Contingency plans
    b. Tactical planning
    c. Executive summary
    d. General objectives

19. How often should management review the long-range plan?
    a. Semiannually
    b. Annually
    c. Biannually
    d. Every three years

20. Which of the following is the company's work plan for the year?
    a. Contingency plan
    b. Strategic plan
    c. Tactical plan
    d. Business plan

CHAPTER 8

Structuring the Organization

■ KEY TERMS

affiliated business arrangements (AfBA)	general partnership	line authority
acquisition	informal organization	merger
chain of command	job descriptions	monolithic organization
corporation	life cycles	profit centers
decentralized organization	limited liability company (LLC)	S corporation
franchise	limited partnership	sole proprietorship
		staff authority

■ LEARNING OBJECTIVES   *When you have completed this chapter, you will be able to*

- **explain** life cycles in a company's development;
- **describe** various forms of legal ownership and modes of operation and **discuss** their advantages and disadvantages;
- **explain** strategies for mergers or acquisitions;
- **explain** the process of developing a company's internal operating structure; and
- **describe** chain of command, line of authority, and informal organization and **develop** a proper job description.

CHAPTER OVERVIEW

The structure of an organization is essentially the framework for a company's operations. Companies need operating structures that support their business plans and group work in a logical and efficient manner. That includes a chain of command that clearly defines the path of decision-making authority.

Companies have different modes of operation depending on where they are in their stage of development or life cycle—birth, growth, midlife or maturity, and decline. With each stage come opportunities and challenges that companies have to embrace to be profitable enterprises.

A fundamental decision is the most suitable form of legal ownership. There are a number of options: sole proprietorship, corporation, S corporation (S corp), general partnership, limited partnership, and a limited liability company (LLC). Each one has legal and tax ramifications that can make one form of ownership more desirable than another, depending on individual circumstances.

A company can also decide whether to go it alone as a completely independent enterprise or whether affiliations—such as franchises, national corporations, local affiliations, affiliated business arrangements, and MLSs—are desirable. The advantages and disadvantages have to be weighed along with the costs versus benefits of such ventures. Companies can also use mergers and acquisitions to accomplish their objectives, a strategy that has to be approached very methodically to be successful.

As a company's scope of work grows, the structure of an organization becomes more complex. This requires a series of steps to properly structure work, job positions, and chain of command—depending on whether the company is a small centralized operation or a monolithic or decentralized organization. Sometimes work also flows outside the formal organization chart.

Job descriptions must be created for each position that explain the following:
- What is the scope of work?
- What are the responsibilities for which the position is accountable?
- Where does the position fit into the chain of command?

A job description forms the basis for identifying the skill sets and talents needed to handle the responsibilities of the position.

CHAPTER 8 QUIZ

1. What is one of the challenges of the maturity stage of any sale organization?
   a. Avoiding any of the new concepts that will threaten traditional business activities
   b. Maintaining the level of profitability to which the company is accustomed
   c. Eliminating conflicts between long-term and new salespeople
   d. Getting the new hires to use the tried and true methods of doing things

2. What is an advantage of being a sole proprietor?
   a. Can personally reap the rewards of being in business
   b. More personal liability
   c. Vulnerability in case the owner becomes incapacitated
   d. Lack of expertise and advice from other stakeholders in the business

3. Three brokers decided to form a real estate company. They want to limit their personal liability as well as insulate the company's profits from taxes. To achieve these goals, they can form
   a. a sole proprietorship.
   b. a limited partnership.
   c. a general partnership.
   d. a limited liability company.

4. An organization that functions as a sole legal entity and has perpetual existence and unlimited owners is
   a. a limited partnership.
   b. a sole proprietorship.
   c. a corporation.
   d. an S corporation.

5. What type of legal ownership is limited to a certain number of shareholders who must pay taxes on their own personal tax returns?
   a. Limited partnership
   b. Limited liability company
   c. Corporations
   d. S corporation

6. A relatively risk-free way to start up a business, provide name recognition, and supply the freedom to be an independent owner with a proven product or service is to
   a. become a franchisee.
   b. join the multiple listing service.
   c. join a national corporation.
   d. form a controlled business arrangement.

7. What is a disadvantage of becoming a franchisee?
   a. Name recognition
   b. Entry and exit fees and monthly referral fees
   c. Purchasing power to assemble cross-marketing strategies
   d. Technical expertise from the franchisor

8. What government agency, if any, requires that franchisors provide extensive information about their franchise in the uniform franchise offering circular (UFOC)?
   a. Federal Trade Commission (FTC)
   b. Department of Housing and Urban Development (HUD)
   c. Department of Justice (DOJ)
   d. No federal government agency mandates franchise disclosures, only state agencies

9. What type of arrangement could become an issue under the Real Estate Settlement Procedures Act?
   a. Franchise offerings
   b. Affiliating with a national corporation
   c. Affiliated business arrangement
   d. Cooperative listing services

10. An existing real estate company plans to expand its geographic territory. An excellent way to do this is to
    a. acquire an existing company already located in the new territory.
    b. open a second office, hiring new salespeople to staff it.
    c. buy into a franchise organization.
    d. form a new company with existing salespeople as the shareholders.

11. One of the riskiest ways to recruit experienced salespeople is to
    a. affiliate with a multiple listing service.
    b. join a franchise.
    c. acquire another real estate company.
    d. require a college degree.

12. What is one of the MOST difficult tasks when acquiring an existing business?
    a. Evaluating its managers
    b. Appraising its value
    c. Assessing the condition of its office equipment
    d. Avoiding rumors

13. An organization's internal structure reflects
    a. the complexity of the company.
    b. the profitability of the company.
    c. the way the work of the business is organized.
    d. the productivity of the company.

14. Since rumors begin to circulate before a merger or acquisition, the transition plan should include all of the following EXCEPT
    a. bribery.
    b. containment.
    c. organization.
    d. launch.

15. When the broker's business expanded, the broker realized that he needed to hire several nonselling staff to support administrative functions. The broker is not yet ready to hire a full-time sales manager. This type of organization is MOST likely
    a. a one-person organization.
    b. a monolithic organization.
    c. a decentralized organization.
    d. a controlled business arrangement.

16. Many organizations today streamline their operations by forming a number of work groups or departments utilizing fewer layers of management. These organizations are called
    a. independent.
    b. monolithic.
    c. decentralized.
    d. informal.

17. The order in which authority travels in an organization is known as
    a. the chain of command.
    b. the line of authority.
    c. the informal organization.
    d. the staff of authority.

18. In a real estate organization, what authority is typically given to the people responsible for contributing directly to the achievement of the company's objectives?
    a. Staff authority
    b. Support service authority
    c. Line authority
    d. Supervisory authority

19. The BEST way to ensure that workers know exactly what to do in the company is to
    a. give them a flow chart of the organization.
    b. give them authority to make decisions.
    c. allow them to be creative.
    d. develop job descriptions for each position.

20. Why do people work outside the formal organizational structure?
    a. Right people are in charge
    b. Work is not properly organized
    c. People are fulfilling their responsibilities
    d. Effective communications

CHAPTER

Structuring Business Systems

Americans with Disability
   Act (ADA)
copyright infringement
hotelling

intranet
Office of Health and
   Safety Administration
   (OSHA)

open office
virtual computing
virtual office

■ **LEARNING OBJECTIVES**   *When you have completed this chapter, you will be able to*

- **explain** how to select and design an office that is suitable for a company's operations;
- **explain** how to plan suitable technology and information systems to support a company's operations and **discuss** how the Americans with Disabilities Act affects the way a company serves the public; and
- **discuss** facilities management, including security and safety issues.

CHAPTER OVERVIEW

Office facilities and business systems have to support the work the company needs to do and the way people work today. Although real estate license laws have certain requirements for physical offices, most work is done off-site. This means a company has to provide the supportive services and technology or information systems necessary to facilitate that work.

When planning physical facilities, a company needs to determine the following:
- What work does the office need to support?
- Where does that office need to be?
- What personnel must be accommodated and what provisions do they need?

The objective is to design an appealing and safe, efficient, and affordable workplace that suits the purpose. That workplace must also comply with a number of laws, including the Americans with Disability Act (ADA) and local zoning.

The heart of today's business systems is the technology that manages information and communications—the hardware and software needed to create, collect, manage, and distribute information. When planning technology, a company needs to determine the following:

- What is the type, scope, and amount of data that must be supported?
- What connectivity and networking is needed to make data useful and accessible?
- What do mobile users need the technology to do?
- What is needed to effectively communicate with the public?
- What internal systems and procedures are needed to manage, protect, and store data?
- What external data management resources should be used?

The objective is to provide efficient, affordable, and secure data management for the company and its personnel and to facilitate communication with the public, including consumers with special needs and varied language preferences.

Managing facilities includes keeping the office clean, safe, well-maintained, and keeping costs under control. In addition to requirements of the Office of Health and Safety Administration (OSHA) and other labor laws, the company has certain practical obligations to ensure that office space is secure and safe for its workforce and its clients and customers.

CHAPTER 9 QUIZ

1. Which is a national trend in the 21st century?
   a. Permanence of a physical office
   b. Office wherever the licensee works
   c. Little use of technology
   d. Less responsibility on the primary broker

2. Which is NOT important when selecting a specific site for a sales office?
   a. Sign visibility
   b. Parking availability
   c. Traffic access
   d. Presence of competitors' offices

3. What should be done to determine the number of salespeople needed to cover overhead and profitability?
   a. Divide the square footage of the office by 100 square feet to determine the number of required salespeople
   b. Calculate desk cost to see how many salespeople are needed to cover costs
   c. Find out how many salespeople are in the main competitor's office
   d. Plan on three to four people per desk

4. Locating a sales office in a fixed site becomes less important when
   a. salespeople are readily available to drive clients anywhere.
   b. the cost of gasoline is less expensive.
   c. energy costs are reduced.
   d. real estate offices expand their geographic view of their business.

5. In a multi-office real estate company, the supervisor of the marketing department should be located
   a. in the main office.
   b. in the location where the manager's staff is located.
   c. where the upper management is located.
   d. close to the supervisor's home.

6. The change in the functions of today's real estate offices has
   a. greatly increased the square footage needed.
   b. greatly reduced the square footage needed.
   c. moderately reduced the need for technological devices.
   d. moderately increased the need for skilled, technological licensees.

7. Most of the broker's affiliated licensees do not work in the office, although, from time to time, they need a desk. What strategy BEST supports the licensee's need for available desk space?
   a. Recruiting
   b. Concierge servicing
   c. Hotelling
   d. Buyer brokerage

8. What law should be considered when selecting an office site and designing the space?
   a. Fair Housing Act
   b. Americans with Disabilities Act
   c. The Real Estate Settlement Procedures Act
   d. The National Do-Not-Call Registry

9. The image of a company's operations is MOST readily identified by
   a. the reception area of an office.
   b. the work area of an office.
   c. the fact that salespeople have individual offices.
   d. the training facilities in an office.

10. The layout of an office should be planned so that
    a. salespeople can share desk space.
    b. salespeople can work with customers at their desks.
    c. the public and work areas are insulated from one another.
    d. the largest number of small desks will fit.

11. The creation, collection, conversion, and retrieval of information is called
    a. data management.
    b. networking.
    c. servicing.
    d. firewalling.

12. It is advisable to select the computer software you intend to use before selecting the hardware because
    a. software is quickly outdated.
    b. it's costly to move wiring for computers after they're installed.
    c. automation is invaluable in today's office.
    d. the software determines what hardware capability is needed.

13. What is installed around selected computer files or systems to protect against intrusion?
    a. Firewalls
    b. Wikis
    c. Blogs
    d. Lock-outs

14. Computer systems can now be even more interactive through
    a. web security.
    b. cloud computing.
    c. managing SPAM.
    d. broadband access.

15. What function should be filled no matter the size of the company?
    a. Connectivity
    b. Outsourced service
    c. In-house technical support
    d. Trojan worms

16. A deaf man who is buying a home asks for a sign language interpreter. What law, if any, requires that the real estate company accommodate this request?
    a. Truth-in-Lending Act (TILA)
    b. Fair Housing Act
    c. Real Estate Settlement Procedures Act(RESPA)
    d. Americans with Disabilities (ADA)

17. One of the primary advantages of using a voice messaging system is
    a. messages and phone numbers don't have to be transcribed.
    b. managers don't have to answer phones.
    c. salespeople can avoid callers.
    d. brokers can monitor the salespeople's callers.

18. Providing real estate documents in languages other than English is required by
    a. the Americans with Disabilities Act.
    b. good business practices.
    c. fair housing laws.
    d. equal opportunity laws.

19. What agency, if any, is responsible for the workplace environment in a real estate company?
    a. Department of Housing and Urban Development (HUD)
    b. Office of Health and Safety Administration (OSHA)
    c. Department of Justice (DOJ)
    d. State department of real estate licensing

20. All of the following should be encouraged by the real estate company for the safety of its staff EXCEPT
    a. separating property keys from addresses.
    b. establishing a code or warning system to alert others of danger.
    c. publishing home addresses in social media.
    d. requiring personal identification from clients and customers before showing them properties.

CHAPTER

10

Structuring the Finances

accrual method	debt financing	liabilities
assets	double entry bookkeeping	owner equity
balance sheet	equity financing	profit and loss statement
cash flow statement	fixed expenses	trust or escrow accounts
cash management plan	general operating budget	variable expenses
cash method	income statement	

■ **LEARNING OBJECTIVES**   *When you have completed this chapter, you will be able to*

- **explain** the purposes of various financial statements;
- **identify** financing sources and their advantages and disadvantages;
- **describe** the preparation of a general operating budget and **explain** the use of different types of budgets to monitor a company's operations; and
- **describe** procedures to protect company assets and financial data.

CHAPTER OVERVIEW

None of the company's systems, processes, or people can accomplish the goals of the business plan unless its financial resources are properly aligned to support that plan. Managers use a variety of financial statements (the financials) to evaluate the company's fiscal condition and manage its money. Each of those statements—the balance sheet, the income or profit and loss statement, and a cash flow statement—captures information needed for prudent financial management.

An important part of financial management is ensuring that resources are available when they are needed. This requires a cash management plan and wise forecasting to project capital expenditures and operating needs so that prudent decisions can be made about debt, equity financing, or both. Although start-up companies are usually very dependent on outside resources, every company relies to some degree on those relationships and needs a financing portfolio that makes a worthy pitch for the enterprise.

A company prepares a general operating budget to indicate how the company intends to allocate its financial resources to support the company's business plan. Projections have to be realistic and based on quantifiable evidence for a budget to be a credible financial management tool. Income is supported primarily by service revenue in a real estate company, which involves price setting decisions and antitrust considerations. The expense side includes certain fixed expenses as well as variable expenses. Companies may prepare other types of budgets, including ones for designated profit centers.

Prudent financial management also includes systems and processes that protect the money and financial data. Generally acceptable accounting principles establish standards or the proper methodology for managing financial ledgers to ensure data is accurate as well as best practices and systems of checks and balances to prevent workplace fraud. Procedures typically address the following:

- Who is permitted access to the ledgers or financial database?
- Who is permitted access to checkbooks and inventories of company assets?
- How are the account receivable and account payable functions handled?
- Who is permitted to approve disbursements and for what amounts?
- How is payroll handled?
- What are the procedures for reconciling bank statements?

These procedures are especially important in a real estate company because the principal broker is additionally responsible for other people's money. State license law may stipulate specific procedures for handling trust or escrow funds.

CHAPTER 10 QUIZ

1. A broker requires a loan to expand the company's operations. As part of the application, the lender requires documents that, taken together, provide a picture of the company's fiscal condition called
   a. balance sheets.
   b. profit and loss statements.
   c. income and expense statements.
   d. financials.

2. The report that provides a snapshot of the organization's general financial position as of the date that it is prepared is called
   a. the income statement.
   b. the balance sheet.
   c. the operating budget.
   d. the cash flow statement.

3. The accounting method that reports entries in the period in which they were paid is called
   a. the cash method.
   b. the accrual method.
   c. the operating method.
   d. the declining years method.

4. Which cost is a variable expense?
   a. Brokerage fees
   b. Rent
   c. Depreciation
   d. Cost of sales

5. Upper management of the brokerage firm wants to know how much money it actually has on hand. What reports receipts and disbursements?
   a. Income statement
   b. Cash flow statement
   c. Balance sheet
   d. Financial projections

6. Which of the following enables a real estate company to make it through a six-month downturn in real estate sales?
   a. Accounts receivable
   b. Accounts payables
   c. Cash on hand
   d. Fixed expenses

7. A company does not have enough money on hand to meet its current obligations. All of the following may be used to help the company survive *EXCEPT*
   a. adding an alternative business.
   b. liquidating assets.
   c. bringing in investors.
   d. borrowing money.

8. A brokerage firm requires additional money for expanding its business, but is *NOT* in a position to take out more loans. In this situation, the firm may consider
   a. debt financing.
   b. selling assets.
   c. equity financing.
   d. taking the firm public.

9. A broker is starting her own company. When estimating her cash flow for starting up, she should plan to be dependent on start-up capital for
   a. 3 months.
   b. 6 months.
   c. 12 months.
   d. 24 months.

10. A broker who is starting her own firm could plan on breaking even within
    a. 6 months.
    b. 12 months.
    c. 3 to 5 years.
    d. 5 to 7 years.

11. When the broker approaches a lender for a loan, the application portfolio normally includes a letter of introduction, a personal financial statement, a budget, and
    a. the company's logo.
    b. a floor plan of the office.
    c. evidence of franchise membership.
    d. a business plan.

12. Which financial document can serve the same purpose as a business plan?
    a. Balance sheet
    b. Income and expense report
    c. Cash flow statement
    d. Budget

13. When forecasting income for the year, begin by multiplying the average home sale price by the number of anticipated transactions. Then calculate gross sales income by
    a. multiplying the gross sales volume by the company's commission rate.
    b. dividing the gross sales volume by the average home sale price.
    c. dividing the gross sales volume by the number of salespeople.
    d. multiplying the gross sales volume by the company's commission split.

14. How should a real estate broker determine the commission that the company charges?
    a. Depends on the state licensing commission
    b. Current rates set by local MLS
    c. Sound business rationale
    d. What other brokers charge

15. What fees are prohibited by the Real Estate Settlement Procedures Act (RESPA)?
    a. Fees added for the sake of additional income
    b. Higher rate of commission
    c. Fees for services
    d. Contingency and performance fees

16. In a real estate company, the cost of sales is
    a. listed as income on the profit and loss statement.
    b. a fixed expense on the profit and loss statement.
    c. the same as company dollar.
    d. all of the transaction expenses.

17. What is the name of the account for saving money for a rainy day?
    a. Depreciated replacements
    b. Reserve account
    c. Anticipated net income
    d. Fringe benefits

18. The process of developing a budget is nearly as important as the final document because it allows management to
    a. review its projections.
    b. rely on past experiences.
    c. shift more costs to its sales force.
    d. avoid making any company changes.

19. A work unit charged with the responsibility for generating a portion of the net income in the general operating budget is known as
    a. a profit center.
    b. a sales office.
    c. a variable budget.
    d. company dollar.

20. What MOST influences the accounting procedures for escrow accounts?
    a. Company's auditor
    b. Computer software program
    c. Licensing law of the state
    d. Company's broker

CHAPTER 11

Business Policies and Procedures

KEY TERMS

code of ethics
employee handbook
ethics

open door policy
personnel procedures
manual

policy and procedures
manual
profession
professional

LEARNING OBJECTIVES

When you have completed this chapter, you will be able to

- **discuss** the evolution of ethics and the principles behind ethics in business; **explain** the development of a company's code of ethics and **illustrate** how ethical and professional behaviors can be institutionalized;
- **discuss** the meaning of professionalism and the development of professional standards; and
- **discuss** the development and implementation of policies and procedures, including associated risks and **identify** critical issues that must be addressed by general business policies and procedures, including those that affect employees versus independent contractors.

CHAPTER OVERVIEW

Companies establish policies and procedures, which are essentially rulebooks that are grounded in the company's philosophy of doing business. These are typically written in several documents—a general policy and procedures manual, a personnel procedures manual, and an employee handbook—to establish models of behavior, direct consistent processes, and ensure compliance with various laws.

A company's code of conduct is one of the most fundamental sets of rules. This describes the company's code of ethics, which evolves from morality, principles, and values. A study of the heart of ethics explains the challenges a company faces in establishing a culture for its organization. A company's code of ethics says these are the principles we live by in our relationships within the company and with consumers and others in the business community. This code of ethics may or may not be similar to codes established elsewhere.

The real estate industry strives to characterize itself as a profession. The question that begs an answer is whether the endeavor rises to the level generally ascribed to a profession. However, anyone can do any job professionally by striving to enhance knowledge and performance. Just as with ethics, professionalism is an elusive concept without prescribed standards of behavior. Companies do this by prescribing standards of excellence, which often become part of a company's pledge to its customers and clients.

Companies commit standards of ethical, professional, and legal behavior to writing. Various manuals are prepared for various purposes but the substance essentially tells people how the company operates and what is expected of the people who work for it. The directives generally revolve around the following questions:

- What are the policies and procedures regarding agency representation, antitrust, equal opportunity, and license law requirements?
- What are the company's employment practices and daily workplace procedures?
- How do employees and independent contractors work?
- How are policies and procedures enforced?

Stated policies and procedures intend to institutionalize behaviors and provide ready answers for many dilemmas faced during normal day-to-day operations. This also helps to resolve conflicts before they arise and provides a risk management tool for the company and its staff.

CHAPTER 11 QUIZ

1. In a real estate company, the person responsible for determining the business philosophy for a company is
   a. an office manager.
   b. a broker or owner.
   c. an individual who works there.
   d. a president of the local trade association.

2. A new broker/owner attended a business planning seminar and liked the policy and procedures manual that another broker shared. The primary reason that the policy and procedures manual developed by the other company will *NOT* be useful for the new company is that it may
   a. be outdated.
   b. be unethical.
   c. not be compatible with your organization's philosophy or business.
   d. not anticipate all of the situations that need to be addressed.

3. A company's policies and procedures should be
   a. oral rather than written.
   b. flexible and change as the organization changes.
   c. protected as confidential information.
   d. followed only by management.

4. Regarding the differences between laws and ethics,
   a. ethics may impose a higher standard for conduct.
   b. laws usually impose a higher standard of conduct.
   c. there are rarely any differences.
   d. ethical compliance is a lot easier than obeying the letter of the law.

5. A company needs to adopt a code of ethics to
   a. define its moral principles, rules, and standards of conduct.
   b. establish a code for terminating people's employment.
   c. designate what is expected of people in their personal and professional lives.
   d. enhance its image in the public's view.

6. A company's code of ethics becomes meaningless when
   a. it is inconsistent with the code of other companies.
   b. it is inconsistent with the code adopted by a trade association.
   c. the organization focuses on the results without regard to the process used to achieve them.
   d. legal conduct is unethical.

7. Where are a company's written rules usually provided?
   a. Employee handbook
   b. Personnel procedures manual
   c. Policy and procedures manual
   d. All of these

8. Similar to the rulebook in a game, the company's rules must also provide
   a. sanctions for offenders.
   b. endorsements by senior management.
   c. exceptions to the rules under certain circumstances.
   d. immunities for people in certain positions.

9. In any organization, it is necessary to have
   a. one set of acceptable behavior.
   b. two sets of acceptable behavior, one for management and the other for those managed.
   c. variable sets of acceptable behavior, depending on the amount of money involved.
   d. rigid standards of conduct that are rarely, if ever, changed.

10. A policy and procedures manual can shield a company from legal liability when
    a. the company does not practice within its established procedures.
    b. procedures that affect independent contractors are written as if they are employees.
    c. it is prepared and adopted after review by the company's legal counsel.
    d. it is rarely, if ever, updated to reflect changes in the law.

11. Real estate license law generally requires the broker to
    a. hire equal numbers of males and females.
    b. ensure that the sales force represents the racial composition of the public it serves.
    c. adhere to common commission rates.
    d. define the company's policy on agency.

12. The real estate company should express its philosophical commitment to equal opportunity in
    a. integrating neighborhoods.
    b. hiring anyone who applies to work at the office.
    c. both housing and employment.
    d. compensation.

13. A real estate brokerage company has the right to expect that all people who work for it, regardless of whether they are independent contractors or employees, comply with
    a. the state's labor laws.
    b. the state's licensing laws.
    c. the local trade association's code of ethics.
    d. the local zoning ordinances.

14. What is the primary reason for real estate license laws?
    a. To protect the public
    b. To articulate the value system and principles that govern each company's real estate practices
    c. To define the "best practices" required in every real estate transaction
    d. To identify the minimum standards of practice for listing and selling properties

15. What is the MOST important factor to ensure that a company integrates ethical practices throughout the organization?
    a. Provide a written code of ethics
    b. Arrange for penalties for actions that do not meet the code of ethics
    c. Ensure that every employee receives the employee handbook
    d. Commit the entire organization to following the code of ethics

16. Of what value, if any, is a policy and procedures manual when two salespeople claim the same commission?
    a. No value; the salespeople will still have to file in small claims court.
    b. No value; salespeople will have to take their dispute to the local association of REALTORS® for resolution.
    c. Great value; a company manual provides ready answers for common dilemmas such as this one.
    d. Some value; if the broker/manager agrees with the answer in the manual.

17. Which of the following general policies affect both employees and independent contractors?
    a. Equal employment policies
    b. Vacation and sick leave
    c. Attendance requirements
    d. Expense accounts

18. In a real estate office, termination policies and procedures apply to
    a. only employees.
    b. only independent contractors.
    c. both employees and independent contractors.
    d. only management.

19. Of the following general policies, which affect only employees and not independent contractors?
    a. Nonharassment policies
    b. Substance abuse policies
    c. Holiday time off
    d. Grievance and termination

20. When a company stipulates procedures that apply to independent contractors, these policies
    a. eliminate the need for independent contractor agreements.
    b. guarantee that their independent contractor status will not be challenged by the IRS.
    c. will include recommendations rather than requirements that certain procedures are followed.
    d. need not be followed by the independent contractors.

CHAPTER 12

Marketing and Advertising

■ **LEARNING OBJECTIVES**   *When you have completed this chapter, you will be able to*

■ **describe** the characteristics of a company's brand;
■ **discuss** the purpose and use of various marketing and advertising strategies
   and **describe** how to create and manage an effective website; and
■ **summarize** legal and ethical considerations in various marketing and
   advertising strategies.

CHAPTER OVERVIEW

Marketing is about packaging and placement—putting a memorable face on the
company and creating an appealing message, then placing or promoting that package in ways that make an impression and generate business. A company does this
by creating an identity or brand, which is established with the company name,
logo, and slogan or signature. Then the company needs a marketing plan: a theme
for its messaging and a coordinated strategy to deliver the company's message in
various venues and engage the audience.

Strategies in marketing plans are driven by purpose, population, and price.
■ What is the purpose of the messaging? (institutional advertising, delivery of
   information, promotion of a property, etc.)

- Who is the target audience? (the demographics, their needs-wants-likes, the media venues they frequent, etc.)
- How many people can be reached for the best price?

Today's marketing and advertising programs are highly dependent on digital media, with even traditional media having a digital component to drive message and information. A website is the digital anchor in a marketing plan but it can also be supported by a variety of other digital media—blogs and social media, apps, and online advertising. Each venue is more or less effective depending on how well it's designed and managed and the degree of audience participation it stimulates.

Traditional print and broadcast media provide advertising opportunities and outlets for press releases and letters to the editor as well as opportunities to be resources for reporters. As with digital media, the effectiveness of these venues depends on the design and delivery of the content. A marketing plan may also incorporate a variety of other promotional tools: brochures, flyers, directories, open houses, yard signs, direct mail, and personal solicitation.

Everything a company and its sales force do is a branding opportunity. This also means the company image or reputation is at stake in every word, action, and interaction with the public. Marketing and advertising activities require considerable managerial oversight to protect the brand and ensure compliance with various laws.

CHAPTER 12 QUIZ

1. A new brokerage firm hires an ad agency to develop the company's signature, which consists of
   a. words, graphics, and colors that give it identity.
   b. the salespeople who work for it.
   c. the broker's reputation.
   d. the advertising tools it uses.

2. What is a fictitious business name (FBN)?
   a. Broker's personal legal name
   b. Company and the franchise name
   c. Name registered in the state for the business
   d. Illegal name for the business

3. Of what purpose is the company's name?
   a. Little value
   b. No value, if the company belongs to a franchise
   c. Valuable, if it is clever and memorable
   d. Valuable, if it tells the consumer about the company's value or service

4. An integrated strategy for using advertising tools is known as
   a. a business plan.
   b. a marketing plan.
   c. a financial plan.
   d. a public relations plan.

5. Which medium is drawing the attention of more buyers than ever before?
   a. Television ads
   b. Newspaper pull-out sections
   c. Websites
   d. Neighborhood newsletters

6. What is the goal of a "purpose, population, and price" advertising campaign?
   a. Pick the venue that reaches the desired population for the best price
   b. Advertise in as many different media sites as possible
   c. Use fewer appearances over longer periods of time to reach more people
   d. Choose as many different venues as possible

7. In addition to designing a website, management must ensure that
   a. people are getting to the site.
   b. salespeople use it.
   c. salespeople answer responses quickly.
   d. people spend at least 15 minutes at the site.

8. When creating content for the company's website, developers should remember that
   a. readers are typically located in the community of the real estate company.
   b. website readers will remember, in stunning detail, long paragraphs.
   c. people will carefully read any well-written message.
   d. people will scan for information.

9. What can be added to ensure that the company website is easily accessible by people who are blind or who have impaired vision?
   a. Include many photos, charts, or graphics
   b. Add text to images
   c. Post documents as PDFs
   d. Use many colors, especially for color-coded displays

10. The primary purpose of establishing a blog is to
    a. avoid customer service problems.
    b. find a listing today.
    c. establish a following.
    d. sign up buyers.

11. Domain names and site contents are
    a. too expensive for the average sales agent.
    b. assets known as intellectual property.
    c. expenses that are difficult to justify.
    d. protected by MLS rules.

12. Which of the following is an example of online advertising?
    a. Banner and video ads
    b. Blogs and Twitter
    c. Company's website
    d. Site management

13. From the public's point of view, a newsletter is an ideal vehicle for real estate licensees to
    a. provide useful information.
    b. express their personal views.
    c. promote their company.
    d. distribute coupons.

14. To maximize its usefulness by the media a press release should
    a. editorialize and present the broker's personal views.
    b. present a commercial for the broker's company.
    c. include the company's signature.
    d. provide information that is useful for the public.

15. A reporter who writes about real estate topics calls the broker for a comment about a recent uptick in sales. How should the broker respond?
    a. Offer to return the call in a few minutes
    b. Provide as much information as quickly as possible
    c. Avoid being quoted in the press
    d. Ask the reporter to email the questions

16. According to research, the most effective print advertising includes all of the following EXCEPT
    a. location.
    b. many abbreviations.
    c. price.
    d. size of property.

17. Which of the following words/phrases is permissible under the Fair Housing Act when writing an ad for the local newspaper that also features its ads on the internet?
    a. Adults preferred
    b. Wheelchair ramp
    c. Good parish schools
    d. Hispanic neighborhood

18. The Telephone Consumer Protection Act prohibits
    a. cold calling.
    b. calling those who have registered on the do-not-call list.
    c. calls to people between 9:00 am and 9:00 pm.
    d. calls after 6:00 pm.

19. Who is ultimately responsible for the accuracy and legality of any company advertising in print or on the internet?
    a. Owner of the listing
    b. Real estate licensee who wrote the ad
    c. Broker in charge of the office
    d. Whoever paid for the ad

20. An ad that says, "a two-bedroom house that is ideal for adults, in a mature neighborhood, near the synagogue," is most striking because it
    a. violates the fair housing laws.
    b. is very descriptive about the house and the neighborhood.
    c. doesn't include a price.
    d. doesn't use abbreviations that would be cheaper.

CHAPTER

13

The Practical and Legal Realities of Staffing

■ **KEY TERMS**

candidate profile

common-law independent contractor

employee

equal employment opportunity laws

exempt workers

harassment

independent contractor (IC)

job analysis

license-in-referral organizations (LIFROs)

nonexempt workers

salaries

statutory independent contractor

variable pay plans

wages

■ **LEARNING OBJECTIVES** *When you have completed this chapter, you will be able to*

■ **explain** how staffing needs and job qualifications are determined, **describe** the various categories of employment positions, and **discuss** the decisions that have to be made about hiring sales personnel;

■ **explain** how compensation plans are developed and administered, including various categories of pay; and

■ **describe** how various state and federal laws affect employment and compensation practices.

CHAPTER OVERVIEW

The organizational process determines staffing needs by considering the work that needs to be done and the job positions that are needed to do it. In today's real estate companies, that generally means employing a number of managerial, administrative, secretarial, and clerical personnel in addition to the sales force. Employment positions are characterized as full-time—exempt or nonexempt— and contingent positions. The latter are the temporary, part-time, or leased

51

workers and independent contractors (ICs). The scope and permanence of the work drive decisions about whether full-time employees or contingent workers are needed to fill the positions. Staffing a sales force requires decisions about the following:

- How many sales people are needed?
- Are they full-time or part-time personnel and how are those definitions characterized?
- Is the company looking for experienced or newly licensed salespeople?
- Are the salespeople employees or are they common-law or statutory ICs?

Companies need a methodical and legally defensible process for selecting, hiring, promoting, terminating, and compensating the workforce. This includes developing a job analysis and candidate profile that describes the knowledge, skill sets, experience, and personal characteristics that are necessary to perform each job and are a business necessity for the company. Compensation planning and administration is a function of the company's philosophy about paying people—entitlement or performance—the position of the jobs within the organization, and the accompanying qualifications and expertise or experience level of the people in those jobs. The point of compensation is to reward people for their value to the company. Companies must adopt a methodical process to convert value into pay in an equitable and just manner and ensure that equal work gets equal pay. Once adopted, pay policies must be publicized.

Pay plans may be wages (hourly rates of pay), salaries (annual rates of compensation), or variable play plans (singular or combinations of base salary, commission, bonuses or other benefit incentives). Compensation for sales and managerial personnel is typically based on some form of variable pay plan. Pay practices must comply with employment laws, including state labor and wage-and-hour laws. The Fair Labor Standards Act may also apply. This is particularly important for administering overtime pay and determining which workers are exempt versus nonexempt.

The sales force is typically compensated with straight salary, straight commission, or salary and bonuses or other performance incentives. Supervisory and managerial personnel are generally compensated based on the level of their responsibility in the organization and the activities for which they are accountable. Typically these are salaried or salary plus performance-based compensation plans.

Employment practices are one of the most litigious areas of business. Every human resource management activity must scrupulously guard against any conduct that violates the rights of people who are protected by the federal, state, or local employment laws. Those laws don't differentiate between independent contractors and employees either. Companies must also adopt anti-harassment policies and comply with OSHA's health and safety requirements.

CHAPTER 13 QUIZ

1. A real estate company wants to ensure that all necessary tasks between contract signing and closing/escrow are completed correctly. The people who provide the company with some quality assurance that transactions will proceed smoothly to closing are called

    a. personal assistants.
    b. extra secretaries.
    c. transaction coordinators.
    d. risk management consultants.

2. A top-producing real estate licensee wants someone to help with non-sales-related clerical tasks related to listings and closings. Who is likely to fulfill these tasks?

    a. A personal assistant
    b. An extra secretary dedicated to the top producer
    c. A transaction coordinator
    d. A risk management consultant

3. What is the problem with using desk costs to determine the required number of salespeople?

    a. Factors in too much profit
    b. Does not accurately portray break-even in the real estate company
    c. Accurately reflects what a new person costs the company
    d. Easy to calculate the benefits of each salesperson

4. A better designation than full-time versus part-time sales staff is

    a. independent contractor.
    b. desk cost.
    c. calculating break-even per salesperson.
    d. establishing minimum production levels.

5. One of the strongest reasons for brokers to consider the employee model when hiring salespeople is

    a. gaining greater control over sales activities.
    b. it is easier to pay withholding taxes and Social Security.
    c. reaping the most income benefit.
    d. being less likely to be charged with wage discrimination.

6. What reason would a company have for wanting to hire newly licensed salespeople?

    a. Do not have to pay as much for their production
    b. Do not have to deal with discontent
    c. Easier to train in the company's way of doing business
    d. Easier to provide a solid revenue base

7. When supervising independent contractors, brokers can

    a. require that they attend sales meetings.
    b. determine their vacation schedules.
    c. expect that they comply with laws that affect the business.
    d. restrict the territory in which they can list properties.

8. When brokers structure the commission program for their salespeople, considering equity with the competition is important because

    a. the salespeople evaluate the broker's program for fairness in comparison with other brokers.
    b. licensing laws require equity with the competition.
    c. antitrust laws require equity with the competition.
    d. management must always seek to protect the company's profit margin.

9. A top producer decided to hire a personal assistant who is not licensed. The top producer pays an hourly rate to the assistant to work two hours a day, five days a week. In this situation, can the top producer pay the assistant as an IC (without paying Social Security, etc.)?

    a. Yes, so long as the assistant keeps accurate hourly records
    b. Yes, because the assistant works only 10 hours a week
    c. No, because the assistant does not have a real estate license
    d. No, because the assistant is working less than 40 hours a week

10. The difference between exempt and nonexempt salaried workers is important when determining
    a. pay scales.
    b. overtime pay.
    c. independent contractors status.
    d. holiday pay.

11. The *BEST* way for a broker to determine the company's commission structure is to
    a. ask the salespeople to find out what the other brokers are charging.
    b. have private lunches with individual brokers to discuss commission rates.
    c. use the MLS membership as a guide.
    d. analyze market conditions, transactions costs, and profit requirements.

12. When determining compensation for independent contractors, brokers have traditionally favored
    a. straight salary.
    b. straight commission.
    c. base salary plus bonus.
    d. draw against commission.

13. One problem with accountability-based compensation plans for managers of real estate licensees is that
    a. managers receive compensation for little or no actual accountable work.
    b. it is difficult to justify paying them when the salespeople are actually doing the work of selling.
    c. they have little control over the variables that affect the performance outcomes of those they supervise.
    d. salespeople resent managers being paid.

14. Equal employment laws apply to
    a. employees and not ICs.
    b. employers who hire over 50 employees.
    c. hiring rather than recruiting practices.
    d. hiring and employment decisions for both employees and ICs.

15. When designing employment applications and interview questions, it is appropriate to ask about
    a. references.
    b. marital status.
    c. family matters.
    d. feelings about working with people who are older or younger.

16. All of the following information is patently irrelevant and should not be included in personnel records *EXCEPT*
    a. number of children in the household.
    b. availability to work on Saturday or Sunday.
    c. childhood background.
    d. income expectations.

17. The Equal Employment Opportunity Commission (EEOC) receives the greatest number of discrimination complaints based on
    a. religion and national origin.
    b. race and gender.
    c. disability.
    d. family leave requests.

18. Management should establish
    a. a race relations policy.
    b. an anti-harassment policy.
    c. methods to determine if the applicant has adequate child care arrangements.
    d. interview policies for determining marital status.

19. Numerous state and local laws have added anti-harassment policies prohibiting discrimination based on
    a. sexual orientation.
    b. creditworthiness.
    c. cultural diversity.
    d. traditional values.

20. When seeking a resolution to a sexual harassment charge, the careful broker will
    a. ignore at least two complaints before taking action.
    b. assume that a charge is accurate.
    c. document in writing all that transpires.
    d. avoid putting anything in writing to reduce a paper trail.

CHAPTER

14

Recruiting, Selecting, and Hiring the Staff

■ **KEY TERMS**

annual rate of attrition	Fair Credit Reporting Act (FCRA)	personnel file
career program		prescreening
consumer reporting agency (CRA)	independent contractor agreement	rating system
		recruiting
	noncompete covenants	recruiting program

■ **LEARNING OBJECTIVES** *When you have completed this chapter, you will be able to*

- **explain** factors that contribute to the company being an employer of choice;
- **describe** the five steps in the employment process and their purposes;
  distinguish between recruiting and selecting personnel, **discuss** factors that contribute to a good and legally proper employment interview, and **identify** other protocol that contribute to choosing the right person; and
- **summarize** methods to find the right people for sales positions.

CHAPTER OVERVIEW

The objective in recruiting, selecting, and hiring is to pick the right person for the position. The most trusted companies are in the best position to be the employer of choice. Turnover is a strong indicator of a company's following, and the company needs to consider what is lacking in opportunities or attractive alternatives that can give it a competitive advantage. Staffing is an expensive proposition so the objective is to hire personnel the company can retain. The employment process is a series of methodical steps—recruiting, prescreening, formal interviews, selection, hiring—that is intended to produce intelligent hiring decisions. Each step is a filtering process, with the objective being to narrow the field of contenders and identify the most suitable candidate for the position.

Each step also has the potential to create legal liability—from the time a job is posted through the screening and interview process to the final selection and hiring process—so the company must establish procedures that are administered fairly and without discriminatory effect. The job description, job analysis, and candidate profile that were previously developed provide the "script" that will keep each step focused on job-relevant criteria. This is especially important for conducting proper interviews.

Companies need an objective process for evaluating candidates. One way to do this is by establishing criteria related to the job description and candidate profile and then scoring or using a rating system to gain a quantitative view of each candidate. Job-skill tests and personality assessments, credit checks, criminal background checks and drug testing may be part of either the final selection or hiring step, depending on the advice of the company attorney. The hiring step generally consists of two steps: the offer and acceptance, and the formal employment paperwork, which may or may not include noncompete covenants. The employment process for the sales staff follows the same steps as for any other position. The objective is to qualify the salespeople the company selects, with quotas figuring into the equation only to the extent that managers analyze recruiting history to determine the number of contacts needed to select the most suitable personnel. Managers must also consider the annual rate of attrition. The real estate industry commonly uses a variety of tactics to generate a pool of recruits. Depending on the talent the company is looking for, tactics answer the following questions:

- What can the company do to recruit experienced talent?
- What can the company do to recruit unlicensed talent?

Companies find that some tactics are more productive than others, and some can create more long-term problems than the short-term benefits warrant. Recruiting is to some degree a competitive sport, but the ultimate objective must be to select the most suitable personnel, especially people who can thrive as independent contractors (ICs) (if that's the company mode of operation).

CHAPTER 14 QUIZ

1. Generally, which is *NOT* a primary consideration when salespeople are selecting a brokerage firm?
   a. Ethics of the firm
   b. Payment for the prelicense school
   c. Clerical support for the agents
   d. Firm's name recognition

2. After the broker initiates a recruiting campaign for more salespeople, the next step is to
   a. hire the applicants.
   b. prescreen the applicants.
   c. conduct a one-on-one interview.
   d. bring the applicants in for an office tour.

3. One of the MOST effective ways for managers to recruit is by concentrating on
   a. recruiting when there is high turnover in their offices.
   b. recruiting at every closing or open house.
   c. increasing commission splits.
   d. increasing the company's visibility in the industry.

4. What is the primary purpose of preliminary interviews and application forms?
   a. Determine the physical ability of applicants to perform a job
   b. Gather basic information to decide whether to pursue applicants
   c. Establish preliminary criteria for reviewing applicants
   d. Show that the manager is meeting recruiting quotas

5. One of the MOST important issues in the prescreening process is that it is
   a. consistent.
   b. brief.
   c. different, depending on the applicant.
   d. supervised by a manager.

6. A script is important during a job interview for all of these reasons *EXCEPT*
   a. that it keeps the interview on track.
   b. that it provides consistency during the process.
   c. that it permits the interviewee to control the interview.
   d. that it ensures that all relevant topics are covered.

7. When the sales manager conducts a formal employment interview, the manager should
   a. concentrate on unfavorable information about the candidate.
   b. sell the company to the candidate.
   c. keep the atmosphere formal.
   d. concentrate on listening rather than talking.

8. After the formal interview, the broker realized that none of the candidates really fit the position. In this situation, the broker should
   a. call back the person who was pretty close to being okay.
   b. return to the recruiting step to find more candidates.
   c. call each person back for another interview and ask another manager to sit in, in case the broker missed something the first time.
   d. hire one of those who applied, and hope for the best.

9. Which is the MOST stressful type of interview?
   a. Simulation or audition interviews, in which the candidate partakes in a problem-solving exercise
   b. One-on-one interviews
   c. Panel interviews, in which the candidate meets with a group of people
   d. Serial interviews, in which the candidate is passed from one person to another

10. A company wants to learn more about a candidate's financial situation. Before ordering a credit check, the company should
    a. be sure that it really wants this candidate.
    b. ask for and receive permission from the candidate.
    c. verify that the candidate holds a green card.
    d. use the information on the application to order the credit check.

11. Under what conditions, if any, may a hiring decision be based on a previous criminal conviction?
    a. If the illegal activity is relevant to the job the person will be doing
    b. Cannot be used against a person who is a member of a protected class
    c. Cannot be used if the person has served time and is not on probation
    d. Cannot be used under any circumstances

12. After the parties come to terms about employment, the next step is
    a. a handshake on the agreements made by both parties.
    b. drafting a written document detailing the agreements.
    c. handing a checklist to the new hire to complete before moving into the desk.
    d. handing the new hire a stack of papers to be signed.

13. A formal offer of employment to an independent contractor should include the conditions of employment including
    a. vacation days.
    b. expected working hours.
    c. a health insurance package.
    d. MLS fees.

14. A clause intended to prevent salespeople from taking valuable company information and contacts to another company is called
    a. the competing clause.
    b. the managerial focus clause.
    c. the noncompete clause.
    d. the noncompletion clause.

15. All of the following information should be contained in the personnel file EXCEPT
    a. who to contact in the event of an emergency.
    b. a copy of a driver's license.
    c. racial identification.
    d. authorization to work in the United States.

16. What is the BEST source of recruiting experienced salespeople from other companies?
    a. Recruiting a manager to bring her salespeople over
    b. Mention changing companies at every closing
    c. Knock the competition at closings and open houses
    d. Encourage your current salespeople to identify others who would be an asset to your company

17. Many people who enter the real estate profession often wish that they had been given more information about
    a. the amount of money that they can make in real estate.
    b. how easy it is to get buyers to sign a contract.
    c. how easy it is to get listings.
    d. how much money and time it takes to be successful.

18. One of the reasons that some educational institutions do NOT permit brokers or managers to solicit their students for recruiting purposes is because
    a. this disrupts the ability of the instructors to recruit for their firms.
    b. students expect to be educated and not recruited.
    c. this disrupts the institutions' ability to hire instructors.
    d. the institutions want to select the firms that the students interview with.

19. The purpose of career programs is to
    a. generate a pool of people to interview.
    b. generate listings.
    c. find buyers.
    d. hire new salespeople.

20. When a real estate brokerage company decides to set up a scholarship program, the company should be involved in the program by
    a. screening the applicants.
    b. determining the scholarship recipient.
    c. setting guidelines for the scholarship award.
    d. hiring applicants who are not awarded the scholarship.

CHAPTER

15

Professional Development

■ **KEY TERMS**

andragogy	mentee	reverse mentoring
brainstorming	mentor	team building
cross training	mentoring programs	retreats
job shifting	orientation programs	training

■ **LEARNING OBJECTIVES**   *When you have completed this chapter, you will be able to*

- ■ **discuss** the process of indoctrinating people into an organization;
- ■ **describe** how a company can develop professional competence, **explain** the strategies that suit the way that adults learn, and **discuss** how a company can make training, mentoring and job-shifting programs effective; and
- ■ **identify** methods by which companies engage people in collaborative efforts.

CHAPTER OVERVIEW

The manager's focus once people are hired is to facilitate their professional development. Today's companies provide a variety of opportunities for their workforces—in one-on-one time with the managers and in the programs that give people the opportunity to learn and contribute to the development of their co-workers and the company team.

This begins with indoctrination, which is a process that acquaints the newcomer with the organization. The person can learn what is expected, including the unwritten practices and subtleties of the office culture. Orientation programs, assessments of new hires, and the development of business plans are also part of the indoctrination process. Developing professional competence is also a process, which includes a variety of things managers do to inspire people as well as the formal programs the company provides. A company has to make wise programmatic decisions, especially about training programs (including sales training programs).

■ What are the business needs that can be addressed with training?

■ Who should be trained and what should they be taught?

■ How should training programs be developed and delivered?

■ What results can be expected and what are the costs versus benefits?

■ What do managers need to do to make training effective?

Training in itself is a process that intends to develop skills, especially those that complement or build on an individual's strengths. Training must be tailored to suit the needs of the trainees and the organization and must be supported or reinforced by the company's policies and procedures and managerial personnel. Another path to professional competence is a mentoring program, which is essentially one-on-one, on-the-job training, typically to complement formal training programs. Although managers play a mentoring role, mentoring programs pair colleagues in formal relationships. These programs have to be structured properly to be effective.

■ Who should be selected as a mentor and as a mentee?

■ How can the company benefit from reverse mentoring?

■ What are mentors and mentees expected to do?

■ How are functional relationships created and conflicts resolved?

■ How is mentoring monitored and what happens when the relationship ends?

Cross training is a version of on-the-job training or a mentoring program that gives people an opportunity to grow beyond their current jobs. Cross-training programs or job-shifting rotations foster teamwork across specialties and departments and help people develop new skills while enhancing morale and retention. This also creates promotable talent. Another way companies invest in professional development is by creating cultures that respect the value of talent and engage people in collaborative efforts. Companies do this with a variety of group-centered activities—problem identification, brainstorming, decision making, attitude and recognition, retreats—each of which requires careful planning and implementation to be effective. The company can also create a culture that encourages people to pursue opportunities outside the organization.

CHAPTER 15 QUIZ

1. The orientation meeting that the manager has with the new salesperson should include
   a. a brief history of the company and its philosophy of doing business.
   b. how to take a listing.
   c. how to hold an open house.
   d. how to work with buyers with very little money.

2. A newly hired sales agent should be encouraged to
   a. decide how many hours to work each week.
   b. develop a business plan.
   c. set up times to consult with their managers.
   d. hand in childcare arrangements, complete with emergency phone numbers.

3. How is professional competence developed?
   a. Strict adherence to the company's business plan
   b. Incorporating the sales staff's business plans into the company business plan
   c. Indoctrination, training programs, mentoring, and job shifting
   d. Letting unproductive people go and hiring more productive salespeople

4. In a real estate sales office, the MOST effective training programs emphasize
   a. any training program that comes along with a proven way to produce outstanding results.
   b. information that contributes directly to the bottom line.
   c. purely knowledge-based educational systems.
   d. a blended-learning focus that concentrates on developing skills or behaviors.

5. What is the difference between education and training?
   a. Training develops skill, and education builds knowledge.
   b. Training develops knowledge, and education builds skill.
   c. Training should precede education.
   d. There really is no difference.

6. The primary purpose of training programs is to
   a. provide insight into the personalities of the attendees.
   b. raise the level of engagement of their workers.
   c. identify job-skill weaknesses.
   d. provide a way to evaluate the performance of workers.

7. What is effective training based on?
   a. Company policies or procedures
   b. Management ideology
   c. Financial resources
   d. A job-skills analysis

8. How can a manager ensure that the training program is MOST effective?
   a. Administer a formal exam at the end of the training program
   b. Compare production before the training and a month after the training ends
   c. Provide follow-up support in implementing post-training skills
   d. Review and analyze post-class evaluations with the trainer

9. When teaching adults, it is important to remember that adults
   a. will accept facts without explanation.
   b. are accustomed to being in a classroom.
   c. are less likely to be anxious or easily embarrassed.
   d. are likely to have experienced physical changes that should be considered.

10. What is one of the problems with the modeling approach to sales training?
    a. Not suitable for inexperienced salespeople
    b. Teaches a script rather than preparing people to think
    c. Assumes that all salespeople will be proficient at both sales and listings
    d. Motivational rather than teaching sales strategies

11. Sales training is MOST effective when salespeople are

    a. taught to get the signatures on the contract as quickly as possible.

    b. removed from the office environment and taught what management thinks they need to learn.

    c. put through the motions but not expected to "buy in."

    d. encouraged to build relationships and relate to people as individuals.

12. What is a benefit of an in-house training program?

    a. Major financial commitment

    b. Requires skilled professional talent to develop and deliver

    c. Requires specific materials and facilities

    d. Presents company's sales tools, business philosophy, and procedures in action

13. Two new licensees and three salespeople from other firms join the company at the same time. How should the manager train these individuals?

    a. Train all five licensees at the same time

    b. Offer basic information to the newly licensed and sharpen stale skills of those already in the business

    c. Offer the same information to each group, but keep them separated

    d. Offer basic information to the newly licensed, but only basic company information to the experienced licensees

14. Which of the following would be a good mentor?

    a. An experienced salesperson who is willing to share

    b. An office malcontent

    c. Someone who is willing to work for free

    d. A person generally available due to lack of production

15. What trend is useful in persuading older workers to learn about marketing and communication in the contemporary business world?

    a. Enroll them in local community college classes

    b. Award prizes for every newly learned technological technique

    c. Reverse mentoring

    d. Conventional mentoring programs

16. The sales manager should be familiar with the training curriculum to

    a. reinforce the suggested activities.

    b. make sure that the trainer is doing her job.

    c. know when to pass the person on to another class.

    d. recognize inappropriate content.

17. The broker is trying to decide if one of the salespeople would be effective as a manager. Which of the following could be helpful?

    a. Asking the manager to mentor the salesperson

    b. Sending the salesperson to management training classes

    c. Cross training

    d. Reverse mentoring

18. What is the manager's role in a problem identification meeting?

    a. Ensure that everyone has an opportunity to speak

    b. Encourage discussion of solutions

    c. Not end the meeting until everyone has had a chance to speak

    d. Evaluate each comment at the time it is offered

19. Twice each year, the manager announces a meeting for the sales staff to discuss ways the company can improve its marketing and advertising program. What kind of meeting is this?

    a. Sales training

    b. Decision making

    c. Problem identification

    d. Brainstorming

20. What is the primary rule during a brainstorming session?

    a. Analyze each suggestion as it is offered

    b. Permit no criticism of the solutions

    c. Limit the suggestions

    d. Allow one person to dominate

CHAPTER 16

Coaching Performance

disciplinary meetings
employee survey
employment-at-will (EAW)
exit interviews

minimum average
    production (MAP)
negative incentives
performance appraisals

performance criteria
personal business plans
psychological contract
self-evaluations

■ **LEARNING OBJECTIVES**   *When you have completed this chapter, you will be able to*

- **compare** the differences between managing employees and independent contractors;
- **explain** how to develop credible performance criteria or standards and **discuss** performance incentives;
- **describe** the performance review process, including the use of rating systems; and
- **discuss** the causes of turnover and resignations and **explain** how to discipline and terminate workers, including the legal issues involved.

CHAPTER OVERVIEW

Coaching is a way to deliver training and foster professional development, and is crucial to retaining good personnel and reducing turnover. The manager's job is also about the elements of personnel management that affect continuing employment decisions and hold people accountable for doing the jobs for which they've been hired.

The goal of human resource management is to forge a psychological contract between the company and the individual workers. The performance of a worker is directly related to the performance of the manager, which means that the company is ultimately responsible for upholding its end of the contract and removing obstacles that hinder performance. That contract is especially significant when supervising independent contractors, which is considerably different than supervising employees.

Performance management is based on performance criteria, which must be clearly related to the job and measurable or quantifiable so that people know exactly what's expected of them, and then using the criterion to monitor performance and make personnel decisions. Personal business plans may reflect the job performance standards as well. The process of developing performance criteria and the continuing feedback managers provide is as important as the end result or the written words.

People deserve the company's acknowledgment of their efforts or performance incentives, which can be provided in a variety of ways, each of which has certain advantages and disadvantages.

The basis of performance appraisals or reviews is the performance criteria or the standards that were developed, and it generally involves a two-step process: rating performance and then a performance interview. Performance must be fairly and equitably assessed (also with as few subjective variables as possible)—generally using some form of a numerical scale or descriptive assessment. Self-evaluations are also useful assessments.

Retention and turnover are essentially the company's (or management's) performance review.

- Does the company realistically portray the jobs when people are hired?
- Did management make good hiring decisions?
- Does the company's work culture foster good employer/employee relations?
- Does the company provide good opportunities for career enhancement?
- Does management respond to the concerns of the workforce and resolve conflicts?

The answers reveal how well the company performs on its psychological commitment to the workforce and where improvements are needed to be the employer of choice. Resignations effectively say the company has failed to deliver on its commitment.

Personnel management also involves less pleasant parts of a manager's job—disciplining a worker and terminating a worker. Even though employment-at-will says the company can hire, fire, demote, and promote whomever it chooses, at-will includes the covenant of fairness and good faith. Disciplinary and termination events require methodical and well-documented procedures to protect the worker from unfair or biased treatment and the company from litigation.

An exit interview is a debriefing session and a time to bring closure to the relationship. These interviews, when conducted properly, provide extremely useful information for the company to evaluate its operations and personnel management procedures.

CHAPTER 16 QUIZ

1. The end result of the independent contractor arrangement with *MOST* real estate licensees is that the company can
   a. recommend and encourage certain behavior.
   b. impose rules regarding vacation days, etc.
   c. require that the salesperson make referrals to the company's affiliated business enterprises.
   d. wonder if anyone is coming to work that day.

2. The way to manage ICs is to
   a. ignore their status and do whatever it takes to reach the company's goals.
   b. be resigned to the fact that they can't be managed.
   c. set production quotas they must achieve.
   d. encourage them and show how they will benefit from management's suggestions.

3. All of the following can be used by a broker to foster better performance *EXCEPT*
   a. efficient company procedures.
   b. career enhancement meetings.
   c. ineffective leadership.
   d. defined job performance activities.

4. What is the primary purpose of a performance interview?
   a. Criticize what a person does
   b. Discuss a person's progress and plans
   c. Identify a person's faults so that he can be corrected
   d. Identify whether a person should be terminated

5. How does a person recognize the standards for satisfactory performance?
   a. By reading the job description
   b. Obtaining positive evaluations from other people in the company
   c. Agreeing with management decisions
   d. Meeting measureable outcomes linked to job performance

6. During the process of developing job standards, the manager should remember that
   a. discussion of past performance is an opportunity to criticize lack of achievement.
   b. overstated outcomes can help push performance.
   c. targets for future performance must be realistic.
   d. the manager sets the standards to meet the overall needs of the company.

7. Evaluating a salesperson's performance in relation to established standards may be done
   a. independently by the manager.
   b. in a group process by others in the office.
   c. by an outside performance testing company.
   d. by a peer evaluation committee.

8. The salesperson is an IC. In this situation, with regards to performance standards, the manager should
   a. insist on the salesperson's agreement to the manager's plans.
   b. gain mutual agreement.
   c. set listing and selling goals for the salesperson.
   d. identify what the salesperson has to do to help meet company financial goals.

9. In a real estate office, who is *MOST* likely to require constant feedback and candid advice?
   a. Millennials
   b. Baby boomers
   c. Established top producers
   d. Those who are meeting their goals

10. How effective are contests and award programs as incentives?
    a. Contests are more effective than award programs.
    b. Both can be harmful unless everyone has a chance to win or be recognized.
    c. Both are suitable for employees but not for ICs.
    d. The licensing laws prohibit tangible prizes but not intangible awards such as recognition.

11. Which is an example of a negative incentive?
    a. Praise in private
    b. Bonuses
    c. Public reprimand
    d. Contests

12. One of the major challenges for a manager when evaluating people's performance is to
    a. find the time to do this.
    b. be fair and objective with each person.
    c. overcome the resentment of independent salespeople.
    d. keep productive salespeople from leaving.

13. Rating performance consists of evaluating actual performance
    a. in comparison with that of the top producer in the company.
    b. in relationship to the standards that were benchmarked as satisfactory performance.
    c. with the performance required to maintain fiscal viability.
    d. tied to subjective evaluations of the worker by the manager.

14. From time to time, management can enhance employee relations and psychological commitment by
    a. conducting exit interviews.
    b. administering an employee survey.
    c. holding brainstorming sessions.
    d. dwelling on faults.

15. If the manager has a problem with something a salesperson has done, the manager should
    a. ignore the problem if the salesperson is an independent contractor.
    b. talk to other salespeople to find out what they think about what the salesperson has done.
    c. address the problem in the next sales meeting to find a solution.
    d. address the problem with the salesperson and agree on a solution.

16. Management announces a new commission structure. Later, when the manager walks into the room, several small groups of salespeople get very quiet. In this circumstance, management
    a. can feel comfortable that the new commission structure meets everyone's approval.
    b. should not feel left out since most people have private conversations from time to time.
    c. should recognize that there may be a real problem regarding the new commission structure.
    d. can safely ignore such signals.

17. When a salesperson walks into the broker's office and announces that he is leaving the company, the broker should
    a. ask the person to clean out his desk immediately.
    b. increase the commission split to keep the salesperson.
    c. inquire about the reason for leaving.
    d. protect her company from sabotage.

18. When a manager asks a salesperson to leave the company, the salesperson should
    a. be surprised.
    b. not be surprised.
    c. expect a second chance.
    d. expect to file a lawsuit.

19. The company's top producer has violated a company policy. The broker had several discussions with the person about this and the salesperson agreed to ways to prevent this from happening again. When the broker learns the problem has reoccurred, the broker's next step is to
    a. consider whether it's appropriate to terminate the salesperson.
    b. exempt the salesperson from the policy.
    c. investigate to see if other salespeople are doing the same thing.
    d. change the company's policy to retain the top producer.

20. A salesperson has made the decision to leave the real estate company. One of the purposes of the exit interview is to learn
    a. the real reason for the departure.
    b. how much the salesperson dislikes the manager.
    c. how much money the salesperson is likely to make at the new company.
    d. what the salesperson is likely to tell the community about the company.

CHAPTER 17

Critiquing Operations

cost of sales	office procedures manual	transaction files
customer service survey	personnel records	vertical growth
horizontal growth	quality service standards	

■ **LEARNING OBJECTIVES** *When you have completed this chapter, you will be able to*

- **describe** methods of managing and using information to monitor the company's activities and **identify** information that should be included in transaction files;
- **discuss** ways to maximize income and minimize expenses; and
- **differentiate** between horizontal and vertical growth.

CHAPTER OVERVIEW

Critiquing operations enables the company to grow by directing resources to the most profitable activities. Managers need information to do this, which requires accurate, complete, and timely data and efficient processes to collect, retain, and deliver that data. This includes procedures that are necessary for legal and regulatory purposes, which is especially relevant to real estate license law. An office procedures manual manages the flow of information and provides security by specifying who has access to what data. In a real estate company, transaction files (listing, sales, and closing activities), license records, and personnel records are especially important.

In addition to the transaction files, the financials and the budget are the most important gauges of the company's performance. Monthly review shows trends in the flow of money and production activity, which is essential for monitoring the company's financial condition and taking corrective actions as warranted. A company can maximize income by identifying the following:

- What business sectors are performing well or create maximum opportunities?
- What, if any, pricing strategies be can be adjusted to maximize income?
- What improvements can be made in the services for buyers and sellers?
- How satisfied are the consumers of the company's services?
- How well does the company handle its public relations and resolve problems?

Management must also be vigilant about monitoring expenses. As a practical matter, a company can cut only so much expense before its business is seriously harmed. The company has to make wise decisions about where to cut and where to spend, which can be done by considering the following:

- How can personnel costs be allocated most effectively?
- Where can marketing and advertising expenses be allocated most effectively?
- How can the costs of sales be allocated to reap maximum benefits?
- Where can economies in office expenditures be achieved?
- How can cash flow be managed more effectively?

Companies strive to grow as a way of growing profits. Meaningful growth is achieved with strategic moves that increase a company's power in the marketplace. Companies do this by growing vertically or horizontally, depending on whether they choose to increase capacity in current core services or business units, or expand their scope of services or venture into new markets.

CHAPTER 17 QUIZ

1. To ensure that management has the necessary information to adequately monitor and evaluate a company's operations, data must be
   a. accurate, complete, and timely.
   b. assembled on a computer system.
   c. assembled by clerical staff.
   d. at least a year old to detect trends.

2. One of the *BEST* ways to prescribe the flow of information and documentation in an office is to
   a. train the support staff to be solely responsible for it.
   b. develop an office procedures manual.
   c. eliminate paper and use computers.
   d. make the bookkeeper responsible for these procedures.

3. The state's licensing law requires that the real estate firm keep detailed records of
   a. the independent contractor (IC) agreements.
   b. the reasons for sales agreements falling through.
   c. the length of time listings are on the market.
   d. the escrow or trust accounts.

4. Which of the following is an immediate red flag that the office has a problem with listings?
   a. Listings are clustered near the office.
   b. There is a large disparity between listing price and sales price.
   c. Buyers are offering above list price.
   d. There are not enough listings on the market.

5. Who is responsible for activities that require a license?
   a. The person performing the activity
   b. The broker
   c. The sales manager
   d. The office manager

6. For which of the following activities should the real estate office have clear written procedures?
   a. The distribution and tracking of referrals
   b. The commission splits for each individual licensee
   c. How to receive a real estate license
   d. The circumstances under which an unlicensed individual can independently hold an open house

7. At what time should management institute strategies to maximize income?
   a. At the end of the year after it is apparent the company did not meet its goals
   b. Only when it is apparent that the salespeople's production is lagging
   c. When the company's accountant recommends this course of action
   d. As an ongoing practice to ensure the company's financial stability

8. The National Association of REALTORS® (NAR) periodically surveys buyers and sellers. The one consistent theme in every report is
   a. the lack of professionalism in the real estate industry.
   b. the importance of satisfaction with a salesperson when making referrals to friends and family.
   c. the lack of integrity and honesty in the real estate transaction.
   d. the importance of paying for referrals.

9. When are quality control procedures *MOST* useful?
   a. They are relevant in manufacturing companies but not in real estate brokerage companies.
   b. The cost of using quality control procedures does not reap sufficient benefit for the company.
   c. The quality of services is more important to the consumer than it is to the company.
   d. Quality control procedures can avoid problems that divert people's efforts from other income-producing activities.

10. One of the MOST important issues to consider when deciding to survey customers is whether
    a. salespeople will resent their customers being surveyed.
    b. other brokerage companies use customer surveys.
    c. the company is willing to act on the information that is gathered.
    d. the company has sufficient computer capability to compile results from the surveys.

11. One of the major sources of dissatisfaction with a real estate company is
    a. miscommunication or misunderstanding.
    b. company cost-containment measures.
    c. from sellers who are annoyed that buyers learn so much from the internet.
    d. from cooperating agents who wanted their offer accepted.

12. Which form of communication is actually the LEAST expensive?
    a. Overnight delivery of documents
    b. First-class postage
    c. Fax materials
    d. Emails with attachments of scanned documents

13. A seller is furious with the listing salesperson, for both the advertising of his home and the manner in which the offer was conveyed to him. Until all the facts are known, how should the company respond?
    a. The salesperson is responsible for calming down the seller.
    b. The manager should back the salesperson.
    c. The manager should pass the responsibility to the responsible broker.
    d. The company, the manager, and the salesperson should not disparage one another.

14. It is six months into the budget year and the manager discovers that the company has already spent 75% of its advertising budget. What is the BEST course of action?
    a. Cease all advertising until the last quarter of the year
    b. Discuss the problem with the salespeople to see if they will assist in advertising costs
    c. Use a courier service
    d. Change the budget to reflect the current pace of spending

15. One simple technique to lower postage costs is to
    a. buy and use a postage scale.
    b. apply an extra stamp to cover any weight issues.
    c. use overnight delivery.
    d. use packages instead of paper envelopes.

16. In the second quarter of the year, the brokers discover that the cost of sales is exceeding the amount budgeted because of the amount of the referral fees that have been paid to date on the sales transactions. What is the BEST course of action?
    a. Monitor the cost of sales for the next three months before making any decision
    b. Lay off support staff
    c. Terminate affiliation with the referral company
    d. Refuse to cooperate on transactions with other brokers

17. What should be done if the company is responsible for paying heating and electric bills?
    a. Comparison shop for the best electric plans
    b. Use prepaid plans for electricity and fuel
    c. Schedule a property inspection
    d. Schedule an energy audit

18. For BEST management of cash, in good times, a real estate company should
    a. upgrade computer equipment.
    b. secure a line of credit.
    c. avoid using the U.S. Postal service.
    d. upgrade the office furnishings.

19. How much working capital should a company have on hand?
    a. One month
    b. Three months
    c. Six months
    d. One year

20. What is the riskiest growth strategy?
    a. Restructure products and services
    b. Venture into new markets
    c. Sell off underperforming units
    d. Cut expenses

CHAPTER 18

Managing Risk

LEARNING OBJECTIVES   *When you have completed this chapter, you will be able to*

- **discuss** the risk to a company's brand and licenses and ways to protect them, **explain** succession planning, and **discuss** cyber security, workplace security, and preparing for a natural disaster;
- **explain** the purpose and processes involved in creating a risk management culture; and
- **identify** defensive strategies for managing risk.

CHAPTER OVERVIEW

Risk is simply a given in the business world, but companies manage risk best by being more proactive than reactive and learning to insulate themselves from threats to their enterprises. There's a sense of complacency that settles in when a company is making money, but threats to the health and well-being of the institution lurk in many places. Companies can protect their enterprises by considering the following:

- What is the company doing to protect its brand?
- What is the company doing to protect the licenses that are critical for its business?

- How will the business continue in the absence of the owner or principal broker?
- What is the company doing to protect its cyber infrastructure and data base?
- What is the company doing to prevent fraud, embezzlement, and data theft?
- How will the company survive a natural disaster?

Companies can protect themselves by creating a risk management culture or a proactive environment that makes risk management a priority and infuses the responsibility for managing risk within everyone in the organization. The process builds offensive strategies by identifying potential threats or anticipating crises and assembling procedures to eliminate or minimize risk to the organization. This is similar to any problem-solving process—identifying, analyzing, evaluating alternatives, and implementing a course of action to handle the risk. An additional offense involves a lawyer, an accountant, and other outside resources.

An important part of a risk management culture creates processes and procedures that can help the organization present a suitable defense should that become necessary.

- Does the company have adequate documentation and record-keeping procedures?
- Does the company have adequate insurance coverage?
- Is the company taking advantage of mediation and arbitration services?

The time, effort, and expense are small in comparison to the cost of loss or civil litigation and damages.

CHAPTER 18 QUIZ

1. The value of a company's brand name is
   a. an intangible asset.
   b. similar to projected earnings.
   c. calculated according to specific industry guidelines.
   d. not likely to affect day-to-day operations.

2. There are many events that can propel a company into a crisis. Which is MOST likely to affect a real estate company?
   a. Principal broker arrested for fraud
   b. Manager in jail because of drug trafficking
   c. Salesperson violates the state license law
   d. Bookkeeper embezzles trust funds

3. What is one of the ways to prepare for the departure of a key player in the organization?
   a. Mentoring pairs for each position
   b. Hire back-ups for each position
   c. Institute in-house training for key positions
   d. Implement cross training

4. The smaller the organization, the more important it is to have
   a. a reorganization plan.
   b. a succession plan.
   c. a plan to replace a disliked manager, if that should occur.
   d. a restructuring discussion.

5. A real estate company must develop policies and procedures that direct the way that their sales agents interface with company files because
   a. most sales agents are not very computer literate.
   b. the company owns the computers and can easily control their use.
   c. most of the mobile devices are owned by the agents, not the company, and are more difficult to control.
   d. the company can repossess the computer or other mobile device when a sales agent leaves the company.

6. What is one simple method to protect company files from computer hackers?
   a. Frequently change passwords
   b. Encourage the use of unsecured wireless networks
   c. Indefinitely retain computer data
   d. Avoid making rules about posting on social media sites

7. In terms of risk management, a company should develop a contingency file of emergency contact information that is
   a. locked in the office with other important information.
   b. carried daily by the manager or broker in charge.
   c. reviewed once a year.
   d. stored off-site.

8. Which is a proactive approach to risk management?
   a. Burden the company with extra procedures that may never be needed
   b. Build offensive strategies by identifying potential threats or anticipating crises
   c. Do nothing if the company has adequate cash reserves
   d. Distract salespeople from concentrating on production

9. Which strategy is MOST effective for managing risk?
   a. Dousing the brushfires as they flare up
   b. Hiding vulnerabilities
   c. Budgeting for costs to bail the company out of problems
   d. Creating a proactive risk-management culture

10. Failing to properly display an equal opportunity notice could be a violation of
    a. antitrust laws.
    b. fair housing laws.
    c. workplace safety laws.
    d. disability laws.

11. RESPA specifically prohibits
    a. kickbacks and certain referral fees.
    b. steering and blockbusting.
    c. price-fixing.
    d. workplace harassment.

12. A company's *BEST* tool to protect itself from various risks relating to customer service is its
    a. business plan.
    b. errors and omissions (E&O) insurance.
    c. policy and procedures manual.
    d. social media efforts.

13. Which sales training technique could be a valuable tool to minimize risk?
    a. Encourage sales people to take short cuts to get the deal done
    b. Allow salespeople to fill in the blanks after the fact
    c. Foster a pattern of behavior in which consumer rights and laws are observed
    d. Engage in practices that contradict the company's ideals

14. Which attitude is *MOST* valuable for managing risk in a real estate office?
    a. See nothing, hear nothing, say nothing
    b. Discover, disclose, document
    c. Buyers are liars and sellers are too
    d. The best deal is the done deal

15. Is there any reason for a broker to maintain any relationship with licensing authorities and fair housing agencies?
    a. They are invaluable resources for clarifying laws as the broker conducts business.
    b. They are adversaries and management should keep its distance from them.
    c. Contacts with them should be handled through the company's attorney.
    d. Their job is to enforce their laws and not provide information.

16. What is the purpose of workers' compensation?
    a. Protect employees against loss of income due to any illness or injury
    b. Pay the company's legal costs to defend a lawsuit
    c. Compensate the company for loss due to the interruption of business
    d. Protect people against loss of income due to injuries sustained on the job

17. What insurance policy covers certain claims against a real estate company because of the professional actions of its salespeople?
    a. Business interruption
    b. Employee practices liability
    c. Errors and omissions insurance
    d. Workers' compensation

18. The disputing parties sit with a person to help with negotiating a resolution to their dispute. This is an example of
    a. arbitration.
    b. mediation.
    c. trial without a jury.
    d. intervention.

19. Is there any value to the use of arbitration?
    a. No, it is more costly to resolve disputes through arbitration than in court.
    b. No, arbitration cannot be used to resolve disputes in real estate transactions.
    c. Yes, it is often less expensive for an arbitrator instead of a judge or jury to render a decision about a dispute.
    d. Yes, the parties in dispute can negotiate a resolution with one another in the presence of an impartial third person.

20. How are *MOST* commission disagreements between brokers settled?
    a. Hearing before a panel organized by a professional real estate organization
    b. Small claims court
    c. Mediation
    d. Arbitration

Answer Key

The answer key contains brief explanations of the correct answer. For further information, refer to the main text, *Real Estate Brokerage: A Management Guide*, Ninth Edition.

Chapter 1 Quiz

1. **b** Today's consumers are more diverse than ever before, with Hispanic, Asian, and women buyers leading the demand.

2. **a** As the magnitude of the subprime mortgage problem emerged, the stock market crashed, thousands lost their jobs, and housing prices dropped 30% wiping out $7 trillion of home-owner's equity.

3. **b** Unlike other business enterprises, real estate companies don't make any products or have any control over the products they sell. So, companies claim rights to products with listings and vigorously control that information.

4. **c** While some technology provides efficient ways to distribute listing information, the internet now provides consumers direct access to information and the ability to drive their own real estate transactions.

5. **d** Now that information can be warehoused, delivered, and exchanged for something of value, the real estate industry has become an information business, more so than a brick-and-mortar one. Its hot commodity is access to property listings.

6. **c** Today's consumers demand a consumer-driven model, which creates products and services to suit consumer demand; this is an outcome of the cyber economy that gives consumers access to most any product, service, or sliver of information with the touch of a key on a tablet, laptop, or smart phone.

7. **a** To appeal to more selective consumers who want to purchase and pay for only selected services, many real estate companies have unbundled their services, shed transaction-based fee structures in favor of alternative pricing models, and now offer a menu of options from which consumers can choose; consumers then pay only for the services they use.

8. **b** State regulators continue to require fixed office locations, but today, consumers are much more interested in what they consume than in where they consume it.

9. **c** Companies can work smarter by hiring salespeople as employees rather than independent contractors because they can exert more control over sales activities. Although employee costs will be higher, ultimately those costs will be offset with higher revenue.

10. **c** Often, companies suffer from an "age divide," a large gap between the younger employees at the lower levels of an organization and the older employees in the top managerial positions. Younger people go where the work is and tend to skip from company to company.

11. **b** Previously, property was expected to appreciate and was viewed as a good investment. Today, despite low interest rates and attractive housing prices, consumers do not expect that housing will appreciate; many have turned to renting instead of homeownership, which has dropped to a 15-year low.

12. **a** Because regulatory law is typically reactive rather than proactive to foster innovation and creative free enterprise, it is not clear how business models will change over time.

13. **c** Most real estate companies are run by baby boomers, the over-age-50 crowd. They are used to doing things the way they have been done in the past and are often resistant to ideas coming from their younger counterparts or from the increasing numbers of Hispanic and Asian consumers.

14. **a** In a traditional MLS, members shared listing information only with other members, as permitted by the property owners who were guided by members. Nonmembers were locked out.

15. **c** IDXs and Virtual Office Websites (VOWs) provide information about listings to everyone, and third-party internet companies sell leads that are generated by the companies' own listings to real estate companies.

16. **d** Although multiple listing service rules are structured to allow the exchange of listing information only between members, many owners whose properties are for sale demand input into those decisions. They expect that the listing

information will be widely disseminated to everyone and anyone.

17. **b** Under a supplier model, the supplier controls the selection of products and services offered in the market place; this practice is known as take-it-or-leave-it. A consumer-driven model creates products and services tailored to suit consumer demand.

18. **c** The real estate industry was once a geo-centric business, but now has few geographic boundaries and is culturally diverse. Hispanic and Asian populations are growing at three times the rate of the overall population, with Hispanics now the largest minority.

19. **d** In some companies, core services can mean linking consumers with job placement for a spouse, day care for a child or elderly parent, or maintenance services. It does not mean that the broker takes any responsibility for verifying the completeness or accuracy of a seller pro-vided property disclosure.

20. **a** In the past, the location of a physical real estate office was a draw for foot traffic. How-ever, in the world of ecommerce, all companies are learning that cyberspace is more important than office space.

Chapter 2 Quiz

1. **a** The essence of leadership is the ability to influence other people and persuade them to follow; we trust that the leader will use power and influence responsibly, will answer to the group as a whole, and will stay the course with-out wavering or changing positions.

2. **c** Duplicity, that is deception and dishon-esty, is not a desired leadership trait. The most revered traits include integrity, honesty, trust-worthiness, loyalty, and respect.

3. **b** People are faithful when they feel their per-sonal needs are being met. Once that devotion no longer reaps those benefits, or we find our allegiance misplaced, we are no longer loyal.

4. **d** Each person has a personal set of values and codes for ethical and moral behavior, all of which are influenced by family, culture, reli-gion, and society. Leaders are expected to be especially honorable and models for others to emulate.

5. **c** We set high standards for our leaders, expecting that their value systems, ethics, and moral codes are especially honorable and mod-els for the rest of us to emulate.

6. **a** When a person uses power to coerce, we obey out of fear rather than respect; that's the ultimate abuse of power. We look to leaders to stand by necessary, but difficult, decisions.

7. **b** A self-assured leader supports followers and does not sacrifice their interests to make the leader look good. We want leaders who are self-less rather than selfish.

8. **d** Sometimes a leader must change direction after making a decision. Leaders should be will-ing to take care of others, be compassionate, and be open-minded.

9. **d** A healthy sense of ego is important for leaders because they can use their confidence and self-respect to engender confidence in their followers.

10. **c** People face a dilemma when their values or standards and those of their leaders are mis-aligned; if the systems and codes of the leader are different from those of their followers, the followers are offended, even outraged, by their leader's behavior.

11. **b** Leaders are effective when they use team building to build coalitions. Coalitions consist of a core that demonstrates to others the merits of following the leader, a participatory process that is more evidence that the people matter.

12. **c** Decisiveness in leaders provides assurance that they have a clear vision of where the group is going. Decisiveness is not as much about decision-making processes as it is about the ability to frame definitive courses of action. Leaders should accept responsibility for their decisions.

13. **a** Accountability is easy when actions pro-duce the desired results or exceed expectations; however, it is necessary for leaders to accept responsibility and to not blame others when decisions and procedures produce undesirable outcomes.

14. **b** In real estate companies, brokers are held responsible for the activities of the licensees who work for them; regulators do not excuse a licensee's ineptitude or a broker's inability to know all of what the licensees are doing as a defense for violations of the law.

15. **c** When delegating tasks for which the leader is ultimately responsible, leaders must let go of the details and trust that the person will decide how to do the task and will get it done.

16. **d** Delegation works best when the right people are identified for the specific work and the delegator lets go of the details. Not conferring the authority to make commitments, using resources or taking other steps that are needed to do the job, is a failure of trust and confidence.

17. **a** Effective leaders are proactive, not reactive, and will nurture the growth and development of others by delegating responsibility, sharing credit, and being concerned about the entire organization, not just her own group.

18. **a** Leaders are people who usually think outside the box, with long-range, independent thinking that looks for creative, more inspired talent; they build trust, regardless of formal positions.

19. **b** Managers are work focused, not people focused. They administer and make the organization run by doing things that keep business on course, with an eye on short-term objectives and bottom-line dollars to achieve or preserve stability.

20. **c** It's the person, not the title that makes a leader. People develop as leaders through observation and introspection, learning how to behave and practicing what they learn. Good leaders invest in, not only their company, but in community activities and social service projects.

Chapter 3 Quiz

1. **b** In a dictatorial environment, the "dictator" speaks and people are expected to respond without questioning the directives. A property manager may be dictatorial with employees, but it is less likely that a broker can affect such strategies with independent contractors as affiliated licensees.

2. **a** An autocratic organization is more humanistic, respectful, and less threatening or adversarial. Managers see their decision making more as a division of labor than an issue of control.

3. **d** Participatory management creates a job-rich environment in which management is still subtly in charge. The manager delegates at least some authority to the person responsible for doing a job.

4. **c** Although laissez-faire style of management is the epitome of a self-directed workplace, it is essentially nonmanagement offering little, if any, guidance. Eventually, the organization may languish into nonexistence.

5. **a** Because the offender may not be aware that her behavior was unacceptable to the manager, the manager should clearly describe the preferred behavior and not attack the person or try to correct every misstep.

6. **b** Behavior is a function of the alternatives that one sees at the time; in other words, behavior is simply a matter of making a choice. The manager can encourage the right behavior by assisting the offender to develop a plan for doing things differently.

7. **b** The manager can reinforce acceptable behavior by offering praise and recognition for desirable behavior. Reinforcement can be a kind word, a pat on the back, or some more formal kind of praise, such as an award.

8. **a** Today's young adults have been described as the "most praised generation." In the workforce, they expect a culture that provides feedback, kudos, and other displays of appreciation to codify worth in the workplace.

9. **d** To cause positive behavioral change, managers can take positive steps such as clearly describing the unacceptable behavior and developing an action plan; however, the most important step to ensure that the behavior has changed is to follow up and hold the offender accountable for implementing the action plan.

10. **c** One of the disadvantages of labeling is that people are often more complex than the label permits, and thus, the manager may not see the person as an individual and may fail to think beyond the label.

11. **c** With today's workforce significantly more diverse than ever before, the manager is likely supervising those whose profile is different from the manager's, thus requiring the manager to learn appropriate behaviors from both a cultural and a legal perspective to properly manage people of differing ages, races, colors, ethnicities, or genders.

12. **a** When managing discussions in an office made up of diverse individuals, the leader's job is to remain a neutral facilitator (not a director of opinion or a devil's advocate), keeping the group focused on the heart of the issue and giving the less opinionated voices a chance to be heard.

13. **b**   Companies can acknowledge diversity with flextime, childcare for working parents, zero tolerance for sexual harassment, and gay-friendly and female-friendly environments. Evaluations should be solely related to job performance, not lifestyle or dress.

14. **d**   When managing-the-manager, the manager must guard against allowing personal events to complicate group dynamics. The manager must learn to carry an immense load of duties and responsibilities, and to do so with calm good humor.

15. **b**   The manager can become a role model in the office by reprogramming attitudes, setting realistic expectations about what can be accomplished, and establishing priorities.

16. **d**   Unless the newly appointment manager has collegiate or corporate experience, she usually needs additional training in business and human resource management. Not everyone with good people skills is good at all the things managers do with people.

17. **d**   Although there may not be a specific singular trait to predict entrepreneurial success, all of the tests do indicate that one of the strongest traits is the confidence that a person has in building a successful business.

18. **d**   Gaining the cooperation of subordinates (and acceptance by the management corps as well) depends on the way that a manager approaches the position, not adversarial or as a popularity contest. Managers gain cooperation by demonstrating genuine respect for the position and the people being supervised.

19. **a**   New managers and their brokers should clearly determine which task, selling or managing, has priority and determine the amount of time and effort that must be devoted to each role.

20. **c**   The full-time sales manager can better supervise the activities of the salespeople, coach their performance, and help them reach their goals without the distraction of competing with the salespeople for leads and personal sales activities.

Chapter 4 Quiz

1. **c**   Because of the sheer volume of email, it is easy for important information to get lost in the shuffle.

2. **b**   Performance reviews or disciplinary problems should be handled in private meetings, not in a public forum.

3. **b**   Group forums are usually preferable for transmitting company decisions that affect everyone.

4. **b**   Wikis are vast repositories of information that, through collaborative efforts, can become a forum where the technical knowledge and skills of a number of people can be coordinated electronically into a useful outcome.

5. **d**   A Really Simple Syndication (RSS) catalogs content from blogs and wikis and delivers it in an easy-to-find fashion. RSS is a huge advantage over emails that get lost in inbox clutter.

6. **c**   Publicizing the meeting agenda can inspire attendance because it shows people that there is actually a plan and it assists them getting into the proper mind-set. The manager should not schedule a meeting unless there is a good reason. Meetings should begin and end on time.

7. **c**   Even with the reliance on electronic communication, managers should still schedule face-to-face meetings when they need to control the delivery of information and receive both verbal and nonverbal feedback.

8. **a**   The least effective public speaking is done off the cuff. Keys to effective public speaking include good planning, picking the right topic, planning an approach, and practicing ahead of time.

9. **b**   Reread the comment or document before hitting send. Instant messages tend to be instant reactions that can have disastrous consequences.

10. **d**   Classic decision making is a deliberate, methodical process involving a set of very rational or logical steps. There is no room for snap comments and quick decisions.

11. **c**   A meeting has to rise above all the competition so that people don't feel that it's another time-wasting exercise. The major culprits to active participation are meetings devoted to information that should have been delivered by a memo or a report.

12. **b**   Face-to-face meetings serve a purpose that can't be achieved otherwise. The most obvious is the ability to share negative information with a number of people at the same time to allow everyone to engage in controlled group discussion.

13. **a** Written communications are preferred to oral when the manager has a lot of detailed information to impart. They should not be used to avoid feedback or meeting with a person face-to-face.

14. **c** Sometimes, disgruntled attention seekers or ringleaders of resistance will attempt to seize the moment to advance their own causes and may come to the meeting with planned opinions, ready to take on the manager.

15. **d** The key to effective public speaking is good preparation, certainly more than can be accomplished in a panicked hour before the scheduled event.

16. **b** Never apologize for your presentation. The message should normally flow beginning with a brief outline of what you intend to cover, then the presentation, and then a review of what you did cover.

17. **b** Corrective decisions resolve problems, dilemmas, or crises that require solutions to keep the organization on track or to maintain order in its systems and processes, in other words, solve problems.

18. **a** Entrepreneurial or institutional decisions involve significant strategic directions, policies, or fundamental systems within the organization. Resource decisions involve the allocation of personnel or money. Mediation decisions are essentially negotiated solutions, primarily involving customer service and personnel issues.

19. **d** The first step in the classic decision-making process is to define the situation by clearly describing the problem or circumstance and the cause or causes. Only then can you begin to consider alternatives.

20. **b** The objective of an effective announcement is to communicate a decision and to enhance the likelihood that it will be implemented. It should not seek to justify and defend the decision or to reopen the topic for discussion.

Chapter 5 Quiz

1. **b** The gross domestic product (GDP) is one of the primary indicators of the general health of the economy, showing the total dollar value of all goods and services produced during a specific period of time.

2. **a** A healthy economy usually generates a low, stable rate of inflation. This trend continued in the United States in the 1990s, but inflation sharply increased to record highs during the Great Recession.

3. **d** Traditionally, to curb inflation, the Federal Reserve has increased interest rates, thus discouraging people from spending and growing the economy. Fewer buyers can afford larger down payments.

4. **a** A large spread between short-term interest rates and long-term bond rates indicates that the Federal Reserve is attempting to fuel the economy by loosening its monetary policy, thus encouraging people to spend and grow the economy.

5. **b** The extraordinary credit boom fostered extraordinary risk-taking that led to issuing billions of dollars in subprime mortgage loans, many of which headed into default in 2007.

6. **a** Business planning during periods of stable inflation often leads people into a false sense of security and results in the inability to quickly make adjustments when the economy tanks.

7. **a** Consumer confidence is affected to a major extent by employment stability and lower interest rates, not convincing real estate advertising or increased environmental regulations.

8. **c** The fundamental challenge in economic growth and development efforts is balancing benefits with costs, not only in terms of money but also in the amount of regulatory intervention that may be involved.

9. **c** The disconnect between the consumer price index and people's checkbooks comes from the fact that measures of core inflation do not include food, fuel, and energy costs—the very prices that have risen dramatically in recent years.

10. **a** Dealers in less-frequently purchased items (vehicles, home appliances, and houses) are more dependent on longer-term sales trends, interest rates, repair-versus-replace, and retrofit-old-versus-buy-new behaviors to judge future business.

11. **d** Consumers are sturdiest when they have job security, wages that are sufficient to support their cost of living, and minimal debt. Low interest rates, which are good for the housing market, are not good for people who rely primarily on investment income for their living expenses.

12. **a** The housing market is one indicator economists agree is a relatively sound gauge of the

strength of the economy, and real estate enterprises are not the only businesses that have a huge stake in the housing market regaining momentum.

13. **b** Both the property owners and real estate industry have been saddled with volumes of regulations and not all are helpful to development; in essence, environmental issues have become real estate issues.

14. **d** The real estate community has always stood firmly on supporting private property rights, believing that too many restrictions limit the rights of ownership and too many controls can discourage development.

15. **d** Regulations that service the public interest can erode the rights of the private owner. Overly aggressive restrictions impede the fundamental rights of ownership, and aggressive controls can discourage development.

16. **d** Most state real estate regulators now require disclosure of agency relationships, disclosure of property conditions, disclosure of environmental substances, disclosure of financing terms, and disclosure of the way that various service providers participate with one another in real estate transactions. However, fair housing laws prohibit disclosures of neighborhood racial composition.

17. **c** The baby boomers, those born between 1946 and 1964, have reached their maximum earning potential. They continue to influence the real estate market as they downsize, relocate, or create multigenerational households.

18. **c** Real estate companies can invest in cultural diversity training to help their agents better recognize and facilitate cultural differences in customs, taboos, and business etiquette.

19. **b** How well a company does is a function of how well management analyzes factors in the local environment that have a bearing on its operations and how pragmatic, and perhaps bold, management is when predicting the future. A company must set its prices to reflect its costs and profit, not based on what other companies charge.

20. **a** Population shifts are driven primarily by employment opportunities, but today's younger generations are also more inclined to explore new venues for their climatic, recreational, or cultural appeal than previous generations were.

Chapter 6 Quiz

1. **a** A market-driven approach for a company's operations helps to ensure that the brokerage provides customers with the location and services that they want.

2. **a** Consumers can be interactive in the pursuit and evaluation of information and can view property listings located almost anywhere.

3. **c** Multiple listing services (MLSs) have merged to form large, regional systems of vast amounts of data that reflect the members' expanded geographic markets and expanded scope of services; most brokerage companies can no longer survive solely on business generated in a highly localized geographic market.

4. **c** Referral networks are useful to serve broader geographic networks, while niche marketing targets very specific or narrow segments of the market with specialized, focused services.

5. **a** While intercity referral networks are attractive, they are only as valuable as the cost-versus-benefit equation allows and if the affiliation can do things that a company and its sales staff cannot do more effectively themselves.

6. **d** A disadvantage of joining an intercity referral network could be the expectation of providing additional services not traditionally provided by the real estate company, including after-the-fact fees to third-party equity contractors.

7. **a** In small or rural markets, a company is more likely to be a generalist, involved with residential sales, land sales, leasing and selling commercial properties, and more. Being a generalist is demanding and requires considerable knowledge about many aspects of real estate.

8. **d** A major drawback to specializing in a niche market is putting all of your eggs in one basket. A downturn in the economy could put the company out of business.

9. **b** Serving real estate investors requires a wide range of expertise about tax laws as well as understanding the current laws governing exchanges when helping people acquire, manage, and dispose of their investments.

10. **a** Real estate counseling requires sophisticated analysis of the investor's circumstances and real estate holdings and then providing educated, objective advice.

11. **b** Designated agency, where permitted by law, attempts to shield the principal broker from dual agency conflicts by allowing the broker to appoint a licensee within the company to exclusively represent only one client while another licensee in the company exclusively represents the other client.

12. **d** Also known as transactional brokerage, nonagency avoids any implication of agency by treating both buyers and sellers as customers in the same transaction. Nonagent licensees have certain statutorily prescribed duties to these customers, but the state law does not consider the duties to rise to the level of a fiduciary.

13. **a** Ultimately, the broker/owner must determine the company's agency policies, and the company must develop services and systems to support those policies.

14. **c** The exclusive-right-to-sell listing is generally preferable to others because it eliminates controversy about whether the listing broker is entitled to a commission. The seller owes the commission no matter who brings the buyer to the transaction.

15. **d** State regulators generally require that real estate licensees explain agency options to ensure that consumers are able to make reasonably informed decisions about the relationships they form with licensees.

16. **a** The broker should study the demographics of the population and the number of various types of properties to determine market segments and services.

17. **b** Tracking the company's market share compared to its competitors provides key pieces of information for gauging company performance, in relationship to its competitors, throughout the year.

18. **c** The marketing team of the franchise company will be happy to discuss statistics and cost comparisons, but visiting with brokers who have relinquished their affiliation with the franchise can offer some very interesting experiences, both good and bad.

19. **d** Before making any decision to expand, the broker should analyze cost-versus-benefits, especially possible affiliations, various marketing strategies, and the ability to attract and retain salespeople. It is important to consider services that other companies offer, not to mimic the competition but to assess the competitive merits of various services.

20. **b** Often, the most valuable tool is the company taking an objective and critical look at all of its current structures, systems, and processes and then applying that knowledge to better meet the needs of the marketplace.

Chapter 7 Quiz

1. **d** The purpose of planning is to better direct the company's human and financial resources to those selected activities that will yield the greatest return on investment.

2. **a** Proper planning is based on specific, measurable goals that provide specific guidance to the organization about the tasks that the organization must do to achieve success.

3. **d** People are more likely to be committed when they see that the plan evolved from a deliberate, logical decision-making process. Engaging people from various levels in the organization not only provides multiple perspectives but also gives people a sense of ownership, which enhances commitment.

4. **c** Planning activities must be integrated throughout the organization to get people to buy into the resulting plan. A plan must be implemented; it serves no purpose being hidden in a drawer.

5. **b** If a plan doesn't materialize as expected during the first year (i.e., the hurricane changes the marketplace), the broker should review the business plan to make adjustments as necessary and set more realistic or achievable goals, given the unexpected circumstances.

6. **c** A typical long-range plan spans three to five years, although many companies have found that three years is better in today's dynamic environment.

7. **d** The mission statement defines the organization's fundamental purpose for existing, the foundation on which the business is built, and, most importantly, forms a vision for its reason for existing in the future.

8. **a** General objectives crystallize on what the organization needs to focus to accomplish its mission in the contemporary environment. Each general objective is supported by a number of specific goals, the end results that the organization wants to achieve.

9. **b** Profitability is not the purpose for an enterprise but rather a validation that the organization is doing the right things in pursuit of a clearly defined mission.

10. **d** This mission statement, "The company is in business to be successful," does little more than hope that the business survives. The goal is not specific, measurable, attainable, or framed in time. A better goal is, "The company plans to be at least third in listing market share."

11. **b** A goal should be specific, measureable, attainable, and framed in time (beginning and completion dates).

12. **b** Strategic planning, also called long-range planning, provides not just goals but also the strategic methodology for accomplishing them.

13. **a** Not all goals are production-related. The strategy part of a plan is where the phase-out of an activity that is no longer suitable is addressed and supported by strategies to assimilate those activities and personnel elsewhere in the organization.

14. **c** Each general objective is supported by specific goals. Each goal is supported by a strategy that prescribes the methodology for accomplishing each goal.

15. **a** A strategy prescribes the methodology for accomplishing each goal. In this case, the goal is to "establish a relocation department." The strategy to reach that goal involves making the necessary preparations and plans to allocate the resources.

16. **b** Contingency plans provide alternatives for the organization in the case of unforeseen events that impact the long-range goals.

17. **b** The executive summary is usually placed right after the table of contents in the formal document, although it is usually written last. It is often a several-page summary that outsiders (lenders and investors) typically see, and as such, captures the essence of the plan.

18. **b** Tactical planning must bring the plan to life by defining activities that are most important and charging people with the responsibility for accomplishing them.

19. **b** A sound, long-range plan becomes the foundation for the company's operations, and an annual review of the long-range plan forms the basis for the next year's plan.

20. **d** The business plan is the company's work plan for the year; it brings together goals and

strategies, including some refinements, and helps to set priorities. Tactical planning directs the workflow under the strategies identified in the business plan.

Chapter 8 Quiz

1. **b** One of the challenges of the maturity stage of any organization is maintaining the level of profitability to which it has become accustomed, let alone growing profit. Unfortunately, the competition and the marketplace may be moving in new directions.

2. **a** The broker who is in business as a sole proprietor can personally reap the rewards of being in business. The sole proprietor is exposed to more liability and cannot benefit from the expertise and advice from other stakeholders in the business. The business is vulnerable if the sole proprietor dies or becomes incapacitated.

3. **d** Limited liability companies (LLCs) are appealing alternatives to S corporations (S corps) and limited partnerships since they limit personal liability while sheltering the company's profits from taxes; the investors are members, rather than partners or shareholders, of the LLC.

4. **c** A corporation is a sole legal entity created under state laws, has perpetual existence, and limits liability of the individual owners. Unfortunately, the corporation pays taxes on its profits and so do the stockholders (i.e., double taxation).

5. **d** The S corporation offers the same first four advantages of a corporation and overcomes one of the major disadvantages, the double taxation, but the number of shareholders is limited. The investors in a limited liability company are members, rather than partners or shareholders, of the limited liability company.

6. **a** Real estate brokers choose to enter into a franchise for brand recognition, technical expertise, and exposure to more clients while still retaining ownership.

7. **b** The cost-benefit is not always apparent, especially the entry and exit fees, monthly royalties, and mandatory advertising costs; additionally, the brand may not have power in a particular marketplace.

8. **a** The FTC requires franchisors to provide a great deal of information about the franchise

in a standardized format, known as the UFOC. Some states have similar requirements as well.

9. **c** An affiliated business arrangement (AfBA) is a network of interrelated companies, owned by one holding corporation, that offer services tied to a real estate transaction. Brokers must use caution when entering into AfBAs to avoid Real Estate Settlement Procedures(RESPA) problems.

10. **a** For the company doing the pursuing, joining forces with another may be the most suitable way to expand operations, gain managerial or staff talent, or gain other assets to strengthen the organization or its position in the marketplace.

11. **c** One of the riskiest ways to recruit experienced salespeople is to acquire another real estate company. Many times, other companies actively recruit the salespeople who are in a company that is being acquired, and they may defect to another company.

12. **b** One of the most difficult tasks when acquiring another company is determining the value of that company. Not all financial records may be available, and some may not be accurate.

13. **c** An internal operating structure is essentially the organization of work performed in that company. As the scope of work grows, the structure of the organization becomes more complex. Work has to be properly organized so the company can work efficiently but, most importantly, provides a structure that motivates and inspires the people who do the work.

14. **a** A transition plan needs to address several issues: containment, organization, and launch. It should not include bribery.

15. **b** A monolithic organization is a highly centralized operation, functioning as a single (mono) unit with the work structured to flow from one source of authority at the top of the organization. The one-person and one- to ten-agent organizations are monolithic in the sense that one person at the top of the organization (e.g., the broker/owner) is the chief in charge of the entire scope of the organization's work.

16. **c** A decentralized organization consists of a number of work groups or departments with fewer layers of management at the top of the organization. They are often viewed as more functionally efficient.

17. **a** The chain of command establishes a formal hierarchy by charting how authority travels and by providing an orderly process for making decisions, issuing instructions, and commanding or directing work.

18. **c** Line authority is given to the people who are responsible for contributing directly to the achievement of the company's objectives; these work groups include the sales offices or the property management, leasing, or new construction departments.

19. **d** Job descriptions state how positions function and convert the scope of authority. They describe the activities for which the person is accountable.

20. **b** People work outside the formal organizational structure when work is not properly organized, when the wrong people are in positions of authority, and when people are not fulfilling their responsibilities.

Chapter 9 Quiz

1. **b** Traditional license laws were rooted in the permanence of a physical office with fixed signage, but in the 21st century, technology allows the office to be wherever people do their work.

2. **d** Today, as companies expand their geographic view of their businesses, the neighborhood sales office becomes less important than the company's ability to interface with consumers electronically. Important considerations when choosing a location for a sales office are sign visibility, parking availability, and traffic access, not the presence of competitors.

3. **b** Calculate desk cost to see how many salespeople are needed to cover your overhead and to generate a profit. Each salesperson typically requires 100 square feet of space.

4. **d** As companies expand their geographic view of their businesses, the neighborhood sales office becomes less important than the company's ability to interface with consumers electronically. When consumers do not have to step inside a physical building for most services, a longer distance to travel on occasion may not be a major deterrent.

5. **b** The supervisor of the marketing department is better off being located in the same place as the staff that person supervises, not necessarily the home office or close to home.

6. **b** The change in purpose of today's office has greatly reduced the amount of square footage needed, but the first consideration of the physical location is the nature of the work it has to support—people, equipment, and public image.

7. **c** With more people working at home who still need to come into the office now and then, hotelling allows them to reserve a workstation for the desired time or work in another office that has availability.

8. **b** Inasmuch as the office provides services to the public, the office must comply with the American with Disabilities Act(ADA). Consider the ADA before selecting the space, not after.

9. **a** The reception area is where the public forms its first impressions of the company and should be calm and inviting, and free of distractions and harsh paging systems.

10. **c** Work space should be separate from the public areas and support an efficient flow of work and the interaction of people and systems.

11. **a** Data management is the creation, collection, conversion, and retrieval of information (data), the most common of which includes word processing, spreadsheet, and financial and accounting functions.

12. **d** A company's computer system is an assemblage of hardware and software components to serve multiple computing purposes for multiple users in a variety of locations. The software often determines the necessary hardware.

13. **a** Firewalls are constructed around selected files or systems to protect against intrusion such as viruses, Trojans, worms, and other intrusions that corrupt files or take over a system.

14. **b** Today's systems are more interactive with cloud computing providing users remote access to data and documents through a web browser, providing storage as well as remote access for synchronizing and sharing files with computers or devices on which the respective software is installed.

15. **c** Even with technical support available from software and hardware companies, someone in-house must be savvy enough to communicate the problem and keystroke through solutions.

16. **d** The ADA requires that real estate companies make accommodations so that people with disabilities can access and partake in the company's services; this may include hiring sign language interpreters, installing a text telephone (TTY), or using large print documents.

17. **a** One of the primary advantages of using a voice messaging system is that messages and phone numbers don't have to be transcribed, thus saving time and increasing accuracy.

18. **b** Providing real estate documents in languages other than English is a good business practice. Not speaking English is not considered a disability under the Americans with Disabilities Act (ADA). Fair housing laws are silent as well.

19. **b** OSHA requires that companies display the OSHA poster and that the workplace environment is comfortable, pleasant, and safe.

20. **c** The staff in a real estate company should protect themselves by guarding the amount of personal information they distribute on their websites and social media sites. Personal identification from customers and clients should be provided before salespeople go into the field with them.

Chapter 10 Quiz

1. **d** The financials are statements that provide a picture of an organization's fiscal condition and consist of the balance sheet, income statement, and cash flow statement.

2. **b** A balance sheet reports the organization's assets, liabilities, and owner equity and provides a snapshot of the organization's general financial position as of the date that it is prepared.

3. **a** The cash method reports entries in the period they were paid, and the accrual method reports entries in the period in which they occurred. The company accountant can assist in determining which method is better for the organization.

4. **d** Cost of sales is an expense. Income is derived from brokerage fees, additional services fees, and transaction fees. Depreciation is any decrease in value of an asset during a period of time, thus affecting the value of the business.

5. **b** The cash flow statement reports receipts and disbursements, which allows the company to know how much cash (money) it has to work with for day-to-day operations.

6. **c** Cash on hand is the liquid asset that fuels a company's operations as opposed to assets shown on the balance sheet that would have

to be traded or liquidated for cash. The greater the cash, the more agile a company can be, thus enabling it to weather downturns in the economy.

7. **a** Cash requirements can be satisfied by liquidating assets or going outside the organization to borrow money or find investors. Each of these alternatives can take time to arrange, cost money, and have lingering consequences that have to be weighed (including possible legal ramifications).

8. **c** The firm can find investors to bring in additional cash for the expansion, as an alternative to borrowing money (debt financing). Although this dilutes ownership interests, the additional cash and expertise may be the prudent method for expansion.

9. **b** A good rule of thumb for estimating the amount of money set aside for operating expenses, especially in the first year, is six months. The first year is the most treacherous, though a company should expect to be totally capital-dependent for at least the first six months.

10. **c** For start-up companies, a three-to-five-year span to the break-even point is a typical projection. In the meantime, companies have to withstand operating losses and may also have to make additional capital expenditures to be competitive.

11. **d** A business plan should be included in any loan application portfolio, as well as a letter of introduction, a personal financial statement, and a budget.

12. **d** General operating budgets serve the same purpose as business plans, that is, they provide a financial road map to keep the organization on track. Budgets are useful if they are realistic in their projections.

13. **a** To calculate gross income, multiply the gross sales volume by the company's commission rate.

14. **c** The broker or owner of the company must decide what to charge consumers based on the cost of providing services, not what other brokers charge. Neither the state licensing commission nor the local MLS may determine rates.

15. **a** Fees added simply to increase income are prohibited by RESPA. Any fee charged by the brokerage must provide a demonstrable benefit to the consumer or an additional real estate settlement service as required by RESPA.

16. **d** The cost of sales includes all the service costs made to assist a transaction to settlement. For most offices, this is one of the largest expenses.

17. **b** The reserve account puts aside money to cover unexpected expenses or to capture opportunities that present themselves.

18. **a** The process of developing a budget is as important as the final product because it forces management to consider and reconsider its projections on income and expenses, allowing the company to make changes if necessary.

19. **a** A profit center is created when a work unit is charged with the responsibility for generating a portion of the net income in the general operating budget.

20. **c** The state license laws most influence the accounting procedures for escrow accounts.

Chapter 11 Quiz

1. **b** The principal owner(s) and senior management are responsible for business philosophy, ethical codes, and policies and procedures, ideally including input from lower levels of the organization.

2. **c** Policies and procedures manuals, personnel procedure manuals, and employee handbooks are all individualized documents, each unique to the business organization that wrote it.

3. **b** Although the rules, once formulated, must be followed by all concerned, they should be revisited from time to time to ensure that they support the organization as it changes and to address issues as they emerge and as laws change.

4. **a** Ethics may impose a higher standard of conduct. Laws tell us what we may not do, not what we should do, and therein lies a big difference.

5. **a** A company code of ethics reflects the cultural values established by the principal owners and senior management for their company, reflecting the company's business philosophy and the principles it values. It does not address issues in their personal lives.

6. **c** The ethical code becomes meaningless if senior management tolerates or ignores behavior that is contrary to the values it has established.

7. **d** All three manuals should address conduct, procedures, and sanctions. The personnel procedures manual is meant for managers, and the employee handbook tells the people who work for the company the day-to-day rules of conduct. The policy and procedures manual is the general operations manual that governs all of the company's operations.

8. **a** The company's rules must also provide sanctions for the offenders, and the rules must have teeth so that people take them seriously and know that there are consequences for digressions. Despite all the written words, the organization is defenseless if the behavior is not consistent with those words.

9. **a** There is no such thing as two sets of acceptable behavior. There should be only one standard to which both management and those managed adhere. Policies and procedures must be revised periodically to support changes in the law, the industry, and the organization and to eliminate outdated or conflicting rules.

10. **c** To avoid legal liability, the policies and procedures manual should be carefully reviewed by legal counsel to ensure that the policies are in compliance with state and federal laws, and that everyone consistently follows the stated guidelines. Rules should be updated as laws change.

11. **d** The broker must clearly define the company's policy regarding law of agency relationships to ensure that the sales force knows how to explain these options to the consumer.

12. **c** The company should express its philosophical commitment to equal opportunity in housing and employment. Fair housing laws never meant that agents were to cause integrated neighborhoods; equal employment opportunity laws do not require that the broker hire just anyone or pay everyone the same.

13. **b** The company policy should state that all of the activities in the organization must comply with the state's real estate license laws.

14. **a** A real estate company must live within the framework of an ever-expanding body of law that intends to protect consumers. The laws explain what is expected of licensees in a legal context, but a company also needs to articulate the value system and principles that govern its business practices so the workers understand what the company expects of them.

15. **d** Once the company adopts a code of ethics and distributes the written copy, the organization must be committed to following the code, requiring the active participation of everyone in the organization.

16. **c** Policies and procedures are especially valuable for providing ready answers for many of the dilemmas people face during the course of daily operations and help to resolve conflicts before they arise.

17. **a** Equal opportunity policies apply to both employees as well as independent contractors. Employees, but not independent contractors, are given vacation and sick leave, expense accounts, and attendance requirements.

18. **c** The company policy and procedures should cover termination policies and convey grievance procedures for everyone, including management, employees, and independent contractors.

19. **c** Holiday time off applies only to employees because, by and large, independent contractors set their own work time frames.

20. **c** The work status of independent contractors should be reaffirmed with careful wording in the company's policies and procedures. Certainly, the company must seek assurance that independent contractors comply with the state license laws; in other situations, such as attendance, the company may recommend guidelines.

Chapter 12 Quiz

1. **a** The company's signature that creates brand name recognition consists of words, colors, and graphics that stick in people's minds.

2. **c** An FBN must be registered in the state and approved by the state real estate regulators before it can be used.

3. **d** The name of the company has to tell the consumer what's unique about the company's value or service; even if real estate is obvious, the company has to distinguish itself from other real estate companies.

4. **b** A marketing plan is similar to a business plan in that it should identify the goals and plan for using the signature to sell the brand and the company's messages.

5. **c** Most buyers are researching properties and prices on the internet several weeks, sometimes years, before contacting a real estate licensee.

6. **a** The goal of purpose-price-and-population is to pick the venue that serves the purpose and reaches the desired population for the best price. For the same amount of money, a short but intense integrated campaign rather than a longer drawn-out one provides greater benefits.

7. **a** Getting people to a site is a major task, and many brokers will pay for placement, a practice called sponsored sites.

8. **d** Websites are compelling because of two things: design and content, written for viewers or users, not readers; and people from all over the world scan, looking for information they want, which may or may not be what was written.

9. **b** Screen readers do not interpret photos, charts, colored-coded displays, or graphics. To ensure that people who are blind or have impaired vision can easily use the company's website, developers should add text to images and post documents in text-based formats, rather than PDFs, which are not accessible to screen readers.

10. **c** The goal of a blog is to establish a following through social media. Blogs are most effective when they inspire consumers to join in the conversation, helping to sell the company with their flattering comments or experiences. They can also provide nearly instant opportunities to acknowledge concerns.

11. **b** Domain names and site content are assets known as intellectual property, which owners frequently protect by copyright and trademark.

12. **a** Although companies often feel that their own websites are their online advertising, as more consumers turn to digital venues, companies turn to banner and video ads—especially when visitor behavior is tracked and analyzed with resulting advertising matched to specific target audiences.

13. **a** A newsletter is most helpful to consumers when it provides useful real estate information about emerging trends, changes in the law, recent court cases, and real estate–related government regulations, while showcasing the company at the same time.

14. **d** A press release must provide information that is useful for the public—such as emerging trends, changes in the law, recent court cases, and real estate–related government regulations—before the media will consider publishing it.

15. **a** The most constructive way to handle media inquiries is to offer to return the call in a few minutes and to use the interim time to compile statistics or other pertinent information and frame the points the broker wishes to make in carefully worded remarks.

16. **b** The most effective print advertising creates a word picture of the property; research indicates that the most important features in an ad are the neighborhood (location), the size of the property, and the price. Avoid excessive abbreviations, especially those that are not common.

17. **b** The fair housing laws prohibit making, printing, or publishing any statement that indicates any preference, limitation, or discrimination based on race, color, religion, sex, familial status, handicap, or national origin. Licensees may affirmatively advertise in favor of people with children or people with disabilities because people without children and people without disabilities are not protected classes.

18. **b** The Telephone Consumer Protection Act protects consumers who have registered to no longer receive unwanted cold calls. The act does not prohibit cold calling, only to those who have registered.

19. **c** The broker in charge is ultimately responsible for the accuracy and legality of any company advertising, whether in print or on the internet.

20. **a** The fair housing laws prohibit making, printing, or publishing any statement that indicates any preference, limitation, or discrimination based on race, color, religion, sex, familial status, handicap, or national origin. The ad violates fair housing laws in two ways: "ideal for adults" and "near the synagogue."

Chapter 13 Quiz

1. **c** Companies hire transaction coordinators to take the burden of tracking transactions from the salespeople to provide the company with some assurance that transactions will proceed smoothly and within the law to settlement.

2. **a** Personal assistants play an increasingly important role in today's real estate business, handling non-sales-related tasks for the salespeople.

3. **b** Desk cost does not accurately portray break-even in the real estate company since it does

not factor in the increased costs involved with a new hire, and it does not factor in profit.

4. **d** Establishing minimum production levels permits the company to use some excellent producers who may have another job.

5. **a** From a company's point of view, the employee model for the sales staff has a number of advantages, most importantly giving the company control over production and better-quality service.

6. **c** Although new licensees require considerable indoctrination, training, and supervision to get them started, they have not acquired any bad habits in the real estate business; it is relatively easy to train a newly licensed salesperson in the company's way of doing business.

7. **c** The employing company/broker is responsible for the independent contractor's (IC's) conduct in accord with real estate license law, but otherwise ICs are free to work wherever and however they choose (within the jurisdictional limits of their licenses). The IC contract typically states some mutually agreed-on amount of production.

8. **a** Equity is important because, in theory, a company can pay people whatever it wants to or can afford. In reality, people do go shopping for the best compensation package.

9. **c** The personal assistant may not be paid as an IC because the arrangement does not meet any of the three tests to determine statutory IC status: have a real estate license, a contract indicating the arrangement, and compensation calculated on transactions completed.

10. **b** The differences between exempt and non-exempt salaried workers is important when it comes to making overtime payments; overtime must be paid to nonexempt salaried workers.

11. **d** The company should base its commission structure on market conditions, transactions costs, and profit requirements; not based on what other brokers pay their salespeople.

12. **b** When determining compensation for independent contractors, brokers have traditionally favored the totally performance-based straight commission; the company reaps the most income benefit, without any obligations for tax withholding or statutory benefits.

13. **c** A flaw in an accountability-based compensation plan for managers in lower levels of the organization is they have less or little control over all the variables that affect the performance outcomes of the office or department they supervise.

14. **d** Equal employment laws do not distinguish between ICs and employees. The applicability of some laws, however, does differ depending on the number of workers a company has and other distinctions that an attorney skilled in employment law can interpret for the company.

15. **a** When designing employment applications and interview questions, it is appropriate to ask about references but not family matters, feelings about working with people of different ages, or marital status.

16. **d** During an interview, an employer may ask about income expectations, but may not gather information that relates in any way to the protected classes such as number of children and child care arrangements, availability on weekends (a religious issue), and childhood background (can reveal nationality and race).

17. **b** The EEOC receives the greatest number of discrimination complaints based on race and gender, although it is clear that no class is immune from employment discrimination in today's culturally diverse workplace.

18. **b** Management should publish an anti-harassment policy that clearly defines behavior that is not tolerated and establish a nonthreatening, open door policy so that the offended person can bring the matter to management's attention without fear of reprisal.

19. **a** In addition to the equal employment laws and fair housing laws, there are numerous state and local laws prohibiting discrimination based on gender or sexual orientation.

20. **c** With any allegation of wrong-doing in the workplace, the careful broker will document in writing all that transpires. The broker should have a zero-tolerance attitude but recognize that not every charge is correct.

Chapter 14 Quiz

1. **b** Salespeople want competitive compensation, clerical support, and a positive work environment in an ethical, recognized firm. Few expect payment for prelicensing.

2. **b** The employment process consists of the following steps, in this order: recruiting, prescreening, formal interview, selection, and the job offer (hire).

3. **d** The company's business reputation and its workplace environment play a vital role in attracting the best people out of the potential candidates.

4. **b** The primary purpose of application forms and preliminary interviews is to gather basic information to decide whether an applicant meets the minimum requirements for the position.

5. **a** The most important part of the hiring process, including the prescreening, is that the company be consistent, ensuring that every inquiry is treated in the same way.

6. **c** A script allows the interviewer to stay on track, ensures that the relevant topics are covered, and illustrates consistency in the interview process. It specifically allows the interviewer, not the interviewee, to control the process.

7. **d** When conducting a formal employment interview, while it is permissible to tell a short story about the company, the purpose of the exchange is to learn about the applicant. Therefore, the manager should concentrate on listening rather than talking.

8. **b** It's possible that no candidates are suitable. If that's the case, go back to the recruiting step rather than waste time with candidates who don't meet minimum qualifications.

9. **a** By their very nature, employment interviews are stressful. The least stressful is a one-on-one interview. There is more stress in panel interviews (the candidate meets with a group of people) or serial interviews (the candidate is passed from one person to another). Simulation or audition interviews are the most stressful, putting the candidate on the spot with a skill demonstration or problem-solving exercise.

10. **b** The company should ask for and receive permission before ordering a credit check. Failure to comply with the Fair Credit Reporting Act (FCRA) can result in civil penalty up to $1,000 and possibly punitive damages.

11. **a** Criminal background checks are appropriate only as long as they are standard operating procedures for all prospective hires. EEOC regulations permit the denial based on a criminal conviction only if the illegal activity is relevant to the job a person would be doing.

12. **b** The use of counsel is drafting a written document that details all of the agreements made between the new hire and the company. Avoid a handshake agreement; memories are faulty and misinterpretations are quite possible.

13. **d** For independent contractors (ICs), the formal offer of employment should include the cost of getting licensed, cost of errors and omissions (E&O) insurance, MLS fees, franchise fees, and other start-up costs. Employees learn about vacation days, expected working hours, and health insurance packages.

14. **c** Noncompete clauses intend to diminish negative impacts by imposing certain restrictions on a worker's future employment. They must be reasonable, and reasonableness varies from locale to locale. Courts uphold very limited covenants in time and geography for independent contractors.

15. **c** At no time is it appropriate to record racial, religious, or national origin information. After the person is hired, certain information may be part of the confidential file and may not be used in management's decision making.

16. **d** Although the best salespeople are highly competitive, a broker's current staff may be the best ambassadors; they are in a position to identify those in other companies who would be an asset in the broker's company.

17. **d** One of the major criticisms about the hiring process in real estate brokerages is that people feel that they haven't been given realistic information about how much time and money is involved to be successful in real estate.

18. **b** People attend prelicense classes for the primary purpose of education, not recruitment. Many educational institutions prohibit active recruitment in class to protect the confidentiality of their students.

19. **a** The goal of career programs is to generate a pool of people to interview, not to promote the company to obtain new listings and buyers. Not every career program will produce interested candidates.

20. **c** The company can commit the funding and set the guidelines for an award based on merit or financial need. The company should allow the educational institution to screen applicants and to determine the recipients.

Chapter 15 Quiz

1. **a** The orientation program should include a brief history of the company; its philosophy of doing business; and internal procedures for handling paperwork, depositing money or escrow funds, and other fiscal matters. Specific job tasks such as how to obtain a listing, work with buyers, and hold an open house come later.

2. **b** Newly hired salespeople, whether recently licensed or experienced, should include developing a business plan.

3. **c** Developing professional competence is a process that begins with indoctrination and continues with a variety of things managers do to inspire the people and the formal programs the company provides.

4. **d** A blended-learning training focus concentrates on developing skills or behaviors to motivate people to adopt certain behavior, process information and experiences, transfer learning into application, and receive support and reinforcement from their managers or supervisors.

5. **a** Education builds knowledge; training develops skill by converting that knowledge into action. Prelicense classes are knowledge-based programs that do not ordinarily develop the actual skills needed to apply that knowledge in daily practice.

6. **b** Training is the general name companies give to programs intended to raise the level of engagement of their workers; salespeople need a wide range of both knowledge and skill to be successful.

7. **d** Effective training is based on a job-skills analysis: to affect behavior in people so they perform their jobs more effectively.

8. **c** Managers play a vital role in what happens after the training program ends. People need their manager's support in implementing their post-training plans, including the feedback that motivates them to use newly acquired skills.

9. **d** Adults are more likely to experience changes in visual, auditory, and motor skills that should be considered by the trainer. They are not likely to accept facts without explanation and are not used to being in the classroom. Of course, many adults and children are anxious in a learning situation and both seek to avoid embarrassment.

10. **b** One of the problems with the modeling approach is that it presumes that the script is fail-safe; it fails to teach the salesperson to listen, analyze, and think on his feet.

11. **d** Sales training is most effective when salespeople learn to build relationships as individuals to deliver personalized services—a business that is a continuum of certain professional, ethical, and legal behaviors.

12. **d** The in-house program allows a company to present its sales tools, business philosophy, and procedures in action. Disadvantages of an in-house program include a major financial commitment for specific materials and facilities, and the necessity of skilled professional talent to develop and deliver the program.

13. **b** Newly licensed training should be separate from those with more experience; it should include basic real estate information and time to develop some field experience. Training for experienced licensees should sharpen stale skills or align skills with contemporary practices and laws, and help them integrate the company's sales practices into their methods.

14. **a** The selection of the appropriate person to be a mentor is critical. The mentor must be experienced, with high professional caliber and skill, and be willing to share with the new person. A person with no production is not a good mentor.

15. **c** Reverse mentoring assigns younger workers an opportunity to mentor their superiors, a way of giving managers and senior executives a fresh perspective and a change to bridge generation gaps. Conventional mentoring typically assigns older or more experienced workers to mentor the younger ones.

16. **a** Managers play a vital role in what happens after the training program ends because there is no lasting effect without follow-through. People need their manager's support to reinforce the suggested behavior in the real world.

17. **c** Cross training gives people an opportunity to grow beyond the jobs they currently do by fostering teamwork across specialties and departments, as well as helping people develop new skills. Cross training not only gives people a chance to test-drive other jobs but also enhances morale and retention.

18. **a** A problem identification meeting creates a forum to gather information but not to suggest

solutions. The meeting should begin and end on time while allowing everyone a limited time to speak.

19. **d** Brainstorming meetings give people an opportunity to tackle a specific problem, tapping into the company's wealth of talent.

20. **b** The primary rule during a brainstorming session is to permit no criticism of any suggestion. The leader should list possible solutions without analysis and encourage as many people as possible to contribute as many ideas as possible.

Chapter 16 Quiz

1. **a** Management cannot impose standards on its independent contractor sales agents, but it can recommend, suggest, or encourage certain behavior. The company can, however, require that the salesperson obey laws that relate to real estate activities.

2. **d** The way to manage ICs is to encourage them and show how they will benefit from management's suggestions.

3. **c** A company is responsible for providing compensation, career enhancement and quality in work life by removing barriers like inefficient company procedures, conflicts among workers, and ineffective leadership that hinders performance.

4. **b** The primary purpose of a performance interview is to mutually understand the results of the evaluation and to plan for the coming year. It is not the time to criticize or terminate.

5. **d** Performance criteria generally have results-oriented and behavior-related components tied to a position's job description and the company's business strategies and priorities. The criteria must focus on the most important aspects of a job and be linked with measurable outcomes so the person knows the standards for satisfactory performance.

6. **c** When developing job performance standards, the manager should use the discussion of past performance to praise and listen to frustrations, and to identify skill competencies that can be incorporated for the coming year. Targets for future performance must be realistic because arbitrary or overstated outcomes set up a person to fail.

7. **a** Either the manager can evaluate a salesperson's performance in relation to established standards or the individual can prepare a self-evaluation; such evaluations are private and should not be performed by a group, a peer, or an outside testing company.

8. **b** Developing personal plans is a team effort, and if the salesperson is an IC, mutual agreement over performance standards is essential.

9. **a** Many millennials expect frequent feedback, candid advice, and counsel from their managers, often in digital exchanges. Older generations are geared to more formal and less frequent performance discussions. Established top producers rarely require much feedback.

10. **b** Generally, companies should try to develop contests and awards that are attainable in some way by almost everyone. One of the problems with using contests and award programs as incentives is that sometimes the same people win over and over again, thus demoralizing the rest of the staff.

11. **c** Negative incentives include embarrassment, reprimand, and criticism as motivation for people to change behavior. At best, these only work momentarily. Some people prefer praise in private and are distressed if their achievements are publically acknowledged.

12. **b** The legal reality of evaluations is they must be clearly job performance based, and fairly and equitably administered for each person. Otherwise, the company can have significant legal exposure.

13. **b** Rating is a process of using a formal methodology to evaluate actual performance in relationship to the standards that were benchmarked as satisfactory performance. Hopefully, it can be objective, not subjective.

14. **b** A very useful and simple way to enhance employee relations is by periodically conducting an employee survey to determine worker's feelings about compensation policies, workplace environment and morale, opportunities for professional development, and more.

15. **d** If the manager has a problem with something a salesperson has done, the manager should identify the problem before scheduling the meeting. They both need to agree that there is a problem, and together, they should develop mutually acceptable alternatives as possible solutions. The manager should document the discussion in writing.

16. **c** Management should take side conversations that cease very seriously, especially when they follow a major announcement that affects the salesperson's money. Management should ask questions carefully, and be ready to recognize that the sales agents may perceive the new commission structure as flawed.

17. **c** When a salesperson walks into the broker's office and resigns, the broker should explore the reason for leaving and where the person is going. While it may not be possible to prevent this loss, the broker should learn about company problems to prevent others from leaving. The broker should not permanently close the door.

18. **b** Once a decision to terminate is made, the salesperson should not be surprised. The grounds for termination should be problem or production oriented and should have been discussed earlier.

19. **a** To show fair and even-handed application of the rules and penalties, the company may have to consider letting even a top producer go. The company should document warnings, evidence of the conduct, etc. Termination is always the last resort.

20. **d** The exit interview is the time to listen to what the person has to say about the manager, the company and, by listening carefully, what the salesperson is likely to say about the company to the community.

Chapter 17 Quiz

1. **a** To ensure that management has the necessary information to adequately monitor and evaluate a company's operations, data must be accurate, complete, and promptly gathered and used.

2. **b** Because so many people handle documents, money, files, and computer input, an office procedures manual should be developed to manage the flow of information; specify who has access to what data and files; and maintain and retain data, files, and records as required by law.

3. **d** The state's licensing law requires that the real estate firm keep detailed records of the escrow or trust accounts.

4. **b** Brokers should be concerned when listings sit on the market longer than the norm, when many listings do not sell, and when there is wide disparity between listing and sales prices.

5. **b** The broker is ultimately responsible for seeing that all license requirements are satisfied, even if the broker has assigned the responsibility to someone else. No one should be permitted to perform activities for which a real estate license is required until that license has been properly issued.

6. **a** The company should have clear procedures (that are publicized and followed) for distributing and tracking referrals, and keep a master ledger as these assignments are made, recording them in each salesperson's file so that authoritative documentation is available. The state dictates how to receive a license and under no circumstances may an unlicensed individual independently hold an open house.

7. **d** Management should institute strategies to maximize income as an ongoing practice to ensure the company's financial stability, not just when the market deteriorates or the company is not meeting projections.

8. **b** NAR periodically surveys buyers and sellers. The one consistent theme in every report is the importance of satisfaction with a salesperson when making future referrals to friends and family.

9. **d** Quality control procedures are most useful when they assist in avoiding problems that divert people's efforts from other income-producing activities, not just in manufacturing companies but also in real estate companies.

10. **c** Companies should only gather information that it intends to act on. Customers appreciate the opportunity to provide feedback, but they become dissatisfied if the company doesn't pay attention to what they say.

11. **a** One of the major sources of dissatisfaction with a real estate company is miscommunication or misunderstandings, which occur when salespeople do not return phone calls or answer emails, and when the clients do not know what the salesperson is doing for them.

12. **d** Today, emails with attachments of the scanned documents is the least expensive, most cost effective, and quickest method of communication.

13. **d** The manager should gather all the facts and talk with the salesperson involved. The company, the manager, and the salesperson must present a united front and not disparage one another in front of outsiders until the matter is resolved with the consumer. If the issue is

suspected to involve legal issues, everyone must avoid making comments without legal advice.

14. **b** Management should monitor the per-contact cost over the course of several months and then rethink the distribution of its advertising dollars. The time may also come to retool the distribution of advertising and promotional costs between the company and the salespeople. Engage the salespeople in solutions; their participation also quells dissatisfaction.

15. **a** A very simple way to economize on postage is to buy and use a postal scale and affix only the appropriate postage. Consider using second-day delivery instead of overnight. Better yet, use email with attached documents.

16. **a** Track referral and franchise fees over a long enough period to determine if there is sufficient added benefit to warrant the expenditure. It may be time to terminate the relationships.

17. **d** If the company is responsible for heating and electric bills, it should definitely contact the local utility company, schedule an energy audit, and act on its suggestions to reduce energy consumption.

18. **b** It is much easier and cheaper to secure a line of credit in good times before lenders get skittish over sagging markets.

19. **c** Companies should have at least six months or more of working capital to weather storms. They should have a line of credit in place before they need it.

20. **b** The riskiest growth strategies are ventures into new markets. The company would be better off selling underperforming units and cutting expenses.

Chapter 18 Quiz

1. **a** The brand name is an intangible asset, as opposed to projected earnings, but it has an enormous effect on a company's position in the marketplace and its future.

2. **c** The real estate company is far more likely to be affected by something one of its sales or broker licensees does in violation of the state license law. While it is possible that the broker could be arrested for fraud, drug trafficking, or even embezzlement, a license law violation is more probable.

3. **d** The people who take on temporary assignments during vacations or other absences of

their superiors, or the companies that have job-shifting or cross-training programs provide readily available talent not just when the unexpected happens but during the normal course of attrition.

4. **b** Any organization, but especially a smaller one, should have a succession plan to assist the organization to rebound should a leader or manager leave for whatever reason.

5. **c** A company must develop an effective, defensive, aggressive security-management procedure and protects all of its data portals, including those in their workers' smart phones, tablets, notebooks, and laptops. Because they aren't typically owned or issued by the real estate company, the company doesn't have the ability to track or disable a device that has been compromised or misplaced.

6. **a** One of the simplest ways to protect company computer files is to frequently change passwords. People should be encouraged to avoid using unsecured wireless networks, and data should be regularly purged from hard drives and portable devices.

7. **d** The company should prepare a contingency file that is stored off-site. It should be updated regularly to ensure that the contact and other information is current and correct.

8. **b** A proactive approach to risk management builds offensive strategies by identifying potential threats, anticipating crises, and assembling procedures to eliminate or minimize risk to the organization.

9. **d** The best defense is to develop a proactive risk-management culture that requires responsibility from everyone in the organization.

10. **b** Failure to display equal opportunity notices could be considered a violation of the fair housing laws. Brokers must ensure that their salespeople treat everyone fairly, without regard to race, color, religion, national origin, sex, familial status, or disability. Some states and municipalities have added protected classes.

11. **a** RESPA specifically prohibits kickbacks and payment of certain referral fees. The fair housing laws prohibit steering and blockbusting, and the antitrust laws prohibit price-fixing.

12. **c** One of management's most useful tools is the company's policies and procedures manual, and it can become clear written evidence about how processes are to work and people are to

behave. The company must be able to demonstrate that it purposely practices what it suggests in the manual.

13. **c** Sales training should be more than how to sell and make money. Training should form a basis for ethical and legal conduct (the legal liability and risk reduction issues) and foster patterns of behavior in which consumer rights and laws are faithfully observed.

14. **b** Today, the best attitude for dealing with risk is to encourage licensees to discover, disclose, and document everything. The days of caveat emptor—see nothing, hear nothing, say nothing—are long gone.

15. **a** Real estate licensing authorities and fair housing agencies are invaluable resources for clarifying laws as the broker conducts business.

16. **d** The purpose of workers' compensation is to protect people against loss of income due to injuries sustained on the job. Business interruption insurance helps a business pay expenses when it cannot operate.

17. **c** The company's errors and omissions (E&O) insurance covers certain claims against the company because of the professional actions of its workers, including its salespeople, who should also have their own coverage.

18. **b** Mediation is a forum in which the parties sit with an impartial mediator and negotiate a resolution to their dispute. It differs from arbitration in that the arbiter(s) take testimony and render a decision, often as binding as a court decision would be.

19. **c** The arbiter (or panel of arbiters) hears testimony from both sides and then renders a decision, which is often as binding as any court decision would be. Arbitration is often speedier and less costly to resolve certain controversies. Mediation allows the parties to negotiate a resolution.

20. **a** Professional real estate organizations frequently offer their members an arbitration forum in which these matters can be settled, which is less costly than going to court. These organizations also provide forums for ethics complaints.